The Duduk and National Identity in Armenia

Andy Nercessian

The Scarecrow Press, Inc.
Lanham, Maryland, and London
2001

SCARECROW PRESS, INC.

Published in the United States of America
by Scarecrow Press, Inc.
4720 Boston Way, Lanham, Maryland 20706
www.scarecrowpress.com

4 Pleydell Gardens, Folkestone
Kent CT20 2DN, England

British Library Cataloguing-in-Publication Information Available

Library of Congress Cataloging-in-Publication Data

Nercessian, Andy.
    The duduk and national identity in Armenia / Andy Nercessian.
      p. cm.
    Includes bibliographical references (p.) and index.
    ISBN 0-8108-4075-8 (alk. paper)
    1. Duduk (Oboe)—Armenia. 2. National characteristics, Armenian. I. Title.
    ML990.D76 N47 2001
    788.5'2'095662—dc21   2001032067

Contents

Acknowledgments v

Part 1: Preliminaries 1

1 Introduction 3
2 Problems of Organology 7
3 The Duduk 17
4 Armenia—A Nation 21

**Part 2: The Centrality of National Identity to
   Perceptions of the Duduk** 27

5 The History of the Development of the Duduk 29
6 The Duduk as Cultural Demarcator 45

Part 3: Context as Prime Determinant of Meaning 51

7 Solo Duduk Playing 53
8 The Folk Ensemble 69
9 Conclusion 81

Appendixes

A Transcriptions and Analysis: The Creation of Mood in
  Duduk Music 85
B A Detailed Description of the Duduk and Duduk Technique 115
C Repertoire 119
D Measurements Employed by Garlen in
  the Construction of Duduks 121

E   Chronology of Major Events Concerning the
     Armenian Nation   123
F   Distribution of the Armenian Population (1988)   125

Bibliography   127
Index   135
About the Author   141

Acknowledgments

My fieldwork benefited greatly from my parents' contacts and friends who were only too eager to help in any way possible. A considerable number of contacts were established on a number of trips my tireless parents undertook in the 1990s, which were certainly troubled years for Armenia. Not only were many of my parents' friends aware of my numerous trips, but in a number of cases went to great efforts to ensure that my time was spent fruitfully and with the most desirable results.

Upon my arrival there, I had the fortune of staying at the home of the head of the AMAA (an Armenian Missionary Association based in the United States that provides help and support for Armenians in difficulty as well as a stable religious community), a Western Armenian, whom I knew from his earlier visits to Greece. This accommodation was very central and ensured that everything I would require was within reach, while securing my freedom to practice the duduk—as no one ever complained.

The good will, talent, flexibility and endurance provided by Vahan Kalstian and Arsen Grigorian made the fruits of this research possible. I would also like to express special thanks to Djivan Gasparyan, Cecilia Prudian, Garlen and all those who with their support made my work a meaningful and thoroughly gratifying experience. Finally, I owe a lot to Henry Stobart, who provided endless hours and much insight for the organization of my material and writing up.

Foreword

Now that we have the whole world at our fingertips, it is ironic that at the same time so much seems to be becoming so carelessly lost and forgotten. Musical cultures and their extraordinary instruments vary unimaginably. Their survival is uncertain and haphazard—everything seems prone to a chaos of conflicting variables, sometimes at the whim of mass inattentiveness.

An instrument may become extinct, its practitioners die out, and it may be condemned to rot in a glass case. At the other extreme, if it's "lucky," it might get picked up by Hollywood and become a star of the New Age. I've never understood why instruments are condemned by Western curators to become artifacts, rather than living things that can be restored or remade and given a continued life.

My interest is that of a composer, but with no desire to borrow and interweave cultural crossovers. I am interested in the pure acoustics—the unsentimental material quality of a tube, a string, a resonator, and so on. Wherever it comes from, it will be special.

Personally, I find the traditional music, untouched by the normalizing effect of Western popular music crossover, more interesting and challenging to listen to. Music is always changing but, I fear, sometimes we descend into a mindless blancmange of globalization.

In a recent work I brought together newly invented experimental instruments I had designed, Renaissance instruments, and instruments outside my own culture. The exercise was one of timbre, less so one of culture. I was privileged to use a duduk made by Varbed Garlen. This deceptively simple, near cylindrical tube of thick rich fruitwood, giving such a special characteristic resonance with its enormous reed, made a special addition to the wind ensemble without romanticizing its place so far from "home." The player was a Western oboist, and there was no attempt to play the instrument in correct Armenian manner.

Andrew Nercessian is in a unique position to advance the true cause of this instrument. He has penetrated the roots of its current practice and history in Armenia in a beautifully thorough and balanced manner, interspersed with entertaining and fascinating accounts of his experiences as musician and researcher. His writings go a long way to understand the relation between musical perceptions between cultures. I strongly recommend musicians of all persuasions have this book on their shelves before it's too late.

Benedict Mason, composer

Part 1

Preliminaries

Chapter 1

Introduction

The *duduk* is a double-reed aerophone made of apricot wood, with a distinctive velvety and deeply evocative sound, which for many Armenians has become strongly associated with notions of national identity. Although almost identical in basic construction to similar instruments played for example in neighboring Georgia (*duduki*), Azerbaijan (*yasti balaman*), and Turkey (*mey*) since the 1920s in Armenia the duduk has slowly acquired a distinctive national identity and sound. Furthermore in recent years the duduk has been brought to the attention of the world through the recordings of Djivan Gasparyan, for example the recording of "I will not be sad in this world" by Brian Eno and the soundtrack to Scorcese's Film *The Last Temptation of Christ* (1988).

On a visit to Armenia in the fall of 1995, I was deeply impressed by the fervour with which a *dhol* (frame drum) player portrayed the duduk as "the most affectionate of instruments," as his favorite *poghain* (wind instrument) and as the most "Armenian of all instruments." Being of Armenian extraction myself but having never lived in the country, such praise and his label of the duduk as Armenian naturally attracted my attention. The very first time I heard of the duduk had been five years earlier in Greece, when someone mentioned how this instrument "had such a power over him." The word "duduk" produced peculiar connotations in me at the time, since in Greece it is usual to speak of a megaphone as a *duduka*, and one usually remembers the megaphone in association with secondhand goods salesmen who drive around the streets of Athens declaring very slowly and in a not highly respected northern accent what is for sale. In addi-

3

tion, I had, as a child, often overheard my parents and grandparents use the word *düdük* in Turkish expressions, which refer to a whistle.

Such conversations are quite common among Western Armenians, under which label my relatives and I may be thought of, who have either never been to Armenia or have only seen it through the eyes of a tourist. Before my visits dedicated to fieldwork, I had taken only short trips to Yerevan, the capital, and had noted differences in our dialects, which initially caused difficulties in communication. Since my first visit in 1993, however, I have absorbed some of the dialectical differences and cultural aspects of life in Armenia.

I was very lucky to have, among some of the friends willing to help in any way possible, Cecilia Prudian, professor of Armenian Music at the Yerevan State Conservatory, whose knowledge of Armenian music history was matched only by her considerable number of acquaintances in all fields of musical activity. It was through her that I met Arsen Grigorian, a duduk player at the *Aram Merangulian* Folk Ensemble, who soon became my teacher. Arsen turned out to have superb teaching skills, many years of experience as a performer in and outside the folk ensemble, and much spare time to satisfy my endless curiosity concerning music and life in Armenia. He was also always happy to drive me around.

Musical life in Armenia is rich indeed, and although in terms of classical concerts, it feels much like home, folk music offers a wealth of new experiences whose meaning is not always clear to outsiders. I attended folk ensemble rehearsals, funerals, weddings, baptisms, concerts, and even a duduk competition. I spent much time with duduk players who were either acquaintances of Arsen or my family, and was able to interview Djivan Gasparyan, who although in his seventies, is highly active as head of *rabis* (a sort of assembly of duduk players who play at funerals), chairman of the jury of a duduk competition, and as an international concert artist continually engaged in recording projects whether for films or for distribution through CDs.

A very special moment in my fieldwork was meeting the duduk maker, Garlen, who is possibly the only maker in Armenia. He showed me a large number of the duduks he had made over the last years, and some of the duduks that he had in his possession, which were at some point played by Levon Madoyan and Vatche Hovsepian, well-known duduk players of the previous generation. Speaking to Garlen was initially not easy since his accent and dialect were unfamiliar to me. Although Arsen who had introduced us was present to translate whenever necessary, our conversations were at first very long and progressed slowly. Garlen very kindly related to me his method of collecting the apricot wood himself from fallen branches, and how his experience at distinguishing "good" wood from "bad" had taken many years to develop. He also showed me some of the machinery he used to ensure that the construction was precise and of high quality.

As my fieldwork proceeded, the association of the duduk with Armenia, and the fact that it affected many aspects of duduk technique, its sound quality, "sadness" and meaning (even the apricot wood from which the duduk is constructed), became increasingly clear to me.

The use of the duduk to express "national feeling" is visible in all realms of duduk activity. These range from the compositional technique employed for the purpose of making the folk ensemble music highly accessible, to the use of the duduk in concerts commemorating certain important events in the history of Armenia for evoking specifically Armenian scenes.

Chapter 2

Problems of Organology

Much of the scholarly material to be found on musical instruments places great emphasis on physical characteristics. Instrument classification has long depended on the means of sound production whence it derives its most basic categorial criteria. The terms *idiophone, membranophone, chordophone,* and *aerophone* are now familiar to all musicologists, and substantiate a framework for the identification of instruments. Such labels provide an introduction for the subsequent descriptions which go on to list the material used in construction, shape, the number of holes or strings, the type of blowing, plucking, strumming involved, possible positioning of hands, tuning, so on and so forth. Even the phrase "organological structure" usually refers primarily to constructional structure. As playing technique and acoustical implications are both dependent and shaped by constructional characteristics, the centrality of concern for such features is understandable.

Such views are in line with the common sense conception of instruments. As with all objects, instruments are held to be something definite, unchanging and stable. In Bronner's words:

> To express themselves people respond quickly with words, but the objects they grasp have more lasting things to say. The object derives power from its fixity. More stable than speech, the object attracts inspection by many senses, especially those of touch and sight. Differences appear in the priority of senses in modern mass society and many older folk societies. (Bronner 1986, 1)

Thus, the importance of physical characteristics outweighs that of acoustical ones, even in such a musically oriented field as musicology.

The preeminence of physical characteristics over acoustical ones in scholarly writing can also be explained through the obstacles raised by any attempt to describe quality of sound and the interaction of different acoustical schemata in words. The idea of pointing out slight traces of oboe-like sounds in the upper register in contrast with the more clarinetty and bassoony sounds of the lower ones, for instance, seems not only absurd, but also irrelevant. With the availability of recordings and other acoustical evidence, there is little need to "describe" sounds. One may easily argue, on the other hand, that there is little need to describe physical characteristics, when one picture can replace so many words. Despite all advances in technology and reductions in cost, including recordings with books is still the exception rather than the rule. Photographs, too, are often expensive to print and encyclopedias, to use a common example, cannot always include photographs.

In reaction to this idea of fixity, which so readily dominates conceptions of instruments, an adaptationist approach has developed in organology. Musicologists and ethnomusicologists have realized that an instrument does not remain the same over large periods of time, it changes. These changes are usually understood through its role in society whence the principle of adaptation comes. The instrument adapts according to the needs of players, audiences, access to constructional resources, etc. The focus remains on physical characteristics, although now, the historical perspective affords insights into the dynamic nature of the conception.

I do not mean to imply that nonconstructional characteristics have not had their place in the organological literature. The symbolicity of instruments, for instance, is always pointed out but retains only a subordinate position to the more reliable physical characteristics. The elusive nature of instrument symbolicity contrasts sharply with the relative stability of its organological structure. Indeed as soon as the focal point shifts from the latter to the former, a whole series of seeming contradictions and complexities arise which can hardly be resolved within the limited theoretical framework available at present, and which therefore threaten to make the nature of the inquiry "unscientific."

The adaptationist approach goes a long way to resolving some of the tensions inherent between a focus on physical structure and one on symbolicity, function or more generally, meaning. As Racy explains:

Adaptational explanations usually treat instruments as organic entities that change in response to different ecological and aesthetic realities. As they migrate or continue to exist in time, they develop in accordance with local sound ideals, visual symbology, construction exigencies, and preferred playing techniques. An adaptational explanation tends to take the musical culture (including performers, instrument makers, listeners, and musical norms) as a vantage point and to recognise the locally determined attributes of musical instruments. (Racy 1994, 37)

He contrasts this with "idiosyncratic observations" which

take into consideration the stable physical properties of certain types of instruments, as well as the performers' natural physiological abilities. (ibid., 37)

Finally, Racy contends that

musical instruments are interactive entities. Being both adaptive and idiosyncratic, they are not mere reflections of their cultural contexts, nor are they fixed organological artifacts that can be studied in isolation from other social and artistic domains. Instead, instruments interact dialectically with surrounding physical and cultural realities, and as such, they perpetually negotiate or renegotiate their roles, physical structures, performance modes, sound ideals, and symbolic meanings. (ibid., 38)

This view conforms to the recent insistence of ethnomusicologists that music is more than simply a medium of social interaction, and we can do more than observe a "reflection of social structures" in it, if this latter theory still stands at all. Indeed, music is a potent social force, and its "medial" qualities are not those of a neutral medium, but one that plays a major role in social structuring and organization.

But to what extent has this replacement of the fixity of an instrument by its "interactive" (to use Racy's words) capacity penetrated into organological thinking? To answer this question, we should first make a distinction between musics and musical instruments, at least in terms of how they have been viewed. Differences in perception have given rise to differences in the respective adaptabilities. A musical instrument is not "music." Conceptions of music have always emphasized its emotive and dynamic potency. Music has never had the problem of being envisaged as some static unchangeable object, which

instruments have had. An instrument is clearly separable into its constituent components of visual shape and sound. The sound of the piano
is different to the shape of the piano. In discourse, the context usually
makes clear which is being referred to. The adaptationist view has
developed out of thinking about the instrument as source of music,
rather than the instrument as artifact. The fixity of an instrument dis-
tinguishes it from a music. This makes it a more reliable transmitter of
history, which, given the right ideological climate, endows it with
great respect as a source of information, in the eyes of musicians and
scholars. This, however, diverts attention from its adaptability, both
constructionally and in terms of meaning. If Racy's perspective has
made it possible for us to challenge the instrument's fixity, it has done
so through a primarily materialist envisagement of the instrument.
And this is my central objection to Racy's view: its materialist limitations and exclusion of analytic potential at the level of meaning.

The presence of a need for a more careful consideration of meaning prompts us to turn to studies of material culture, which have, since
the late eighties been drawn to the concept of artifact polysemy. Although such studies may have a lot to gain by turning to the example
of musical instruments, let us see, for the moment, how we may bene-
fit from an understanding of some of their basic premises, which have
been derived from (to some extent) anthropological scholarship.

Anthropologists have long known the fetishistic possibilities inherent in objects. The numerous examples of fetishism that anthropology has presented have turned scholarly attention to a way of examining objects which are not in the stricter sense of the word fetishes.
Objects are treated as are people and the person-object relationship is
in many ways comparable to person-person relationships. Viewing a
musical instrument as a person makes it a part of the social structure.
Musical instruments may be seen as actively engaging in social interaction, and constitute an important element in social organization.

From the material culture studies perspective, musical instruments are not only important agents defining self and others, they are
influential in how people are perceived. A man with a Steinway in his
house may cause a number of reactions in his first time visitors. They
may decide that he is a "cultured" man, or a "lover of music." If the
man plays the piano well, or gives the impression of being able to do
so, he may convey an air of perfection. The piano's role in doing so is
not passive, since the fact that this man is a perfectionist may not find
expression so immediately in any other form. The man thus acquires a
certain social position defined by an instrument.

Taking another example, Berliner quotes the text of a story song which describes the *mbira's* (an idiophone) "association with the spirit world" among the Shona people of Zimbabwe:

> There was a man who lived in the pool, and in that pool there was a rock in the middle. This man was a great mbira player and travelled all over playing his mbira. He reached one of the villages where there was a very beautiful girl named Hazviemurwi which means "something which cannot be admired." This girl was so captivated with the music of the mbira player that she fell in love with him. (Berliner 1978, 49)

In fact this story depicts much more than a mere "association" between the mbira and the spirit world. The mbira constructs the man who lived in the pool. The girl is the one who seems a passive agent in their falling in love.

This form of interaction is not only evident on a small scale. Instruments often play a highly important role in defining entire peoples and cultures. This is as much the case with the bagpipe of Scotland as it is with the duduk of Armenia. The instrument's appearance and sound are both seminal in the construction of place and culture. For the diasporan Armenian, the duduk may help keep alive a memory of his ancestors whom he never knew. Simply touching or seeing this "ancient" instrument may bring him closer to an imagined past and homeland. To the enthusiast of world music, the sound of the duduk may influence the necessary acoustical as well as visual elements necessary to portray some exotic landscape. Within Armenia, the duduk might provide the urban population with an awareness of the surrounding rural land and culture.

Thinking of musical instruments in the large-scale context of an entire society or culture, however, is problematic. Adaptationist approaches are helpful in overcoming the problem of the supposed stability of an instrument over a period of time. On the other hand little consideration is spared for the instrument's synchronic polysemy within society. Adaptationism in organology is based on the implicit assumption that an instrument plays only one role in society—that is, has a *position*. In fact, if instruments may be thought of as occupying any position at all in some sort of social structure, this thought must contradict itself by acknowledging that they can only really occupy multiple positions. And in so doing, the coherence of the idea of instrument is lost altogether. Perhaps the great obstacle has yet again been this idea of the fixity of the instrument as artifact. Racy's theory on finding a middle way between the adaptational and idiosyncratic approaches still makes no room for multiple meanings that the single constructionally unique instrument is capable of, simply because any polysemy transcends Racy's materialist analytic basis. This limitation obstructs any theoretical framework which acknowledges the truth of the fact that even if playing technique, physical construction, and acoustical components of an instrument remained identical, they could provide the listener with completely different meanings dependent almost entirely on context. Ethnomusicological reports often give the impression that there are a limited number of contexts in which an instrument may be encountered because they are concerned with over-all structures and social forces, rather than what may be thought of as "unique" cases. The latter seem to attract a lot more attention when we are examining our own culture, not surprisingly, as when we speak of the genius of Mozart or the depth of Brahms. Yet in so doing, they are sacrificing precision for the sake of coherence, something which even our so-called postmodernist way of thinking cannot wholly defend.

The complexity of meanings and their relationships to objects and subjects are best examined from a semiological perspective. Nattiez, in his study of Inuit throat games and Siberian throat singing provides us with a model for understanding the relationship between instruments and meaning. Having demonstrated the phylogenesis of circumpolar culture, Nattiez concludes through the failure of a functionalist approach to explaining the *raison d'être* of certain sonorous symbolic forms, that the signifier (for our purposes the sound of the instrument and/or its visual dimensions) "best resists transformation through time" while the signified are "evanescent" (Nattiez 1999, 414).

This view demonstrates what Nattiez calls the semiological autonomy of signifiers and signifieds in symbolic forms, which is an intrinsically anti-adaptationist approach taken from Racy's perspective. Perhaps the word "anti-adaptationist" is misused here, since the subject of adaptation is not the same in the two models. What makes Nattiez's perspective so valuable is the insight that Racy's model may be used for the "meaning" of the instrument rather than the instrument itself in a way that may contradict the original theory. The study of throat games and singing in circumpolar culture tends heavily towards Racy's "idiosyncratic" extreme, as Nattiez contends that the signifier resists transformation through time.

> We find around the pole one stable sonorous signifier characterized
> by the "panting style"—inhalation/exhalation—with the frequent

use of throat-sounds. When the cultural environment changes, the meanings associated with these techniques and gestures change also. Among the Inuit, this vocal technique is used in the context of games, without, apparently, any religious connotation today. Among the Chukchi, it is integrated into the context of ritual dance songs. When the religious overtones are associated with the use of this vocal technique, the signified referred to by the choreography and the vocal sounds varies according to the cultural religious context: the geese, the seals, and natural elements among the Inuit; the bear among the Ainu; a large range of animals among the Chukchi. (1999, 414)

It is the signified that adapts to the needs of the signifier, not vice-versa. Meaning may thus adapt to the idiosyncraticity of the musical instrument.

In effect, the two theories are not really contradictory at all. Nattiez provides us with insights for the one extreme of Racy's dialectics. This extreme, however, is the one I would like to emphasize for dealing with the problem of intrasocietal synchronic polysemy. The same instrument may generate so many meanings (dependent upon context) that the preeminence of one or other of these meanings within society needs to be explained.

A Context Sensitive Polysemy Model

Qureshi, in her study of the Indian *sarangi*, recognizes the significance of multiple meanings and bases her article on the thesis that an instrument is a form of embodied knowledge. For Qureshi, instruments "mean" by permeating cultural knowledge with physicality (in terms of construction) and affect (in terms of sound). Both are subsumed under the general idea of "embodied knowledge" (1997, 2). An instrument is thus a way of retaining cultural memory. Although Qureshi goes on to list a large number of associations that the sarangi has accumulated over the years, how these meanings are actually "released" is not clearly articulated.

To be sure, Qureshi's account is subject-sensitive, that is, it takes into consideration, through the notion of "embodied cultural knowledge," the identity of the listener or viewer of the instrument, but fails to address the dynamics of the relationship between members of a given culture and this embodied knowledge. That every sign derives its meaning from its context as much as from its interpreter is fundamental to all semiotic thinking, and prompts us to pay equal attention to context if we are to understand how cultural knowledge is conveyed via the instrument (its embodiment).

I prefer to think of meaning derived from instruments not in terms of a web of connotations, but to privilege certain meanings more than others, this privilege being (within a given social group) dependent on context. Thus we may separate an instrument's meaning, sometimes produced through affect and sometimes not, into denotations and connotations determined through context. Although it is often the case that the thin line between denotation and connotation is blurred, this should not deter us from recognizing the validity and usefulness of such an approach in a large number of cases. It is precisely cultural knowledge that enables a separation between denotation and connotation in a given context.

But meaning is also heavily dependent on discourse. In some sense, language belongs to the same category of embodied cultural knowledge that instruments and music find themselves in. Language takes affect or feeling, removes it from context to give it generality and assigns a symbol for it. Words and sentences are therefore embodied knowledge. Although the evocative power of language may not in many cases match that of music, its generality and context independence allows it to organize feeling and feeling structures.[1] This is how, in effect, "general" notions of the meanings of instruments are developed and the context sensitivity of an instrument's feeling activating capacity is lost in the conceptualization of the instrument. It is this premise which allows us to adopt the stance that meaning is constructed by language dependent on other forms of embodied knowledge including instrument and music.

Qureshi believes that "the physical sensation of sound not only activates feeling, it also activates links with others who feel." Especially in the case of "imagined communities" such as nations, this link is activated not only through feeling, but also through discourse. It may be true that two people who have never met may establish a link based on aesthetic considerations and the similarity of their reaction to a given music, but how can each one know "who" the other is without discourse? Who are the members of his social group? Is the aesthetic community defined by aesthetics alone? This metaphor challenges the validity of general notions of instruments which don't take into consideration the use of language in the construction of meaning.

My point is that cultural embodiments are first decontextualized and generalized and then appropriated to create general notions. This is the case with instruments and is aptly demonstrated by the duduk. The duduk seems able to provide a huge number of meanings, each dependent on context, but the overwhelming predominance of its symbolicity of national identity is evident (through language, of-course) when Armenians are questioned about the significance of this instrument. In funerals, duduks embody sadness; in certain urban con-certs, rurality; in competitions, quality; in folk orchestra concerts, "au-thentic folk culture." All these meanings are appropriated through language in the notion of a distinctive national identity. Sadness is thought of as a typical attribute of Armenianness, rurality as the es-sence of Armenianness, and quality as the worthiness of Armenian-ness. There can thus be no doubt that the duduk is "truly" Armenian. Historical considerations and associations are not free of this process, but whether they are remembered or not depends on their adaptability to the mainstream general context-insensitive conceptualization.

The idea that music is a means of retaining cultural memory may have great significance for politics, social and cultural formations, and the like. However, the above argument points to a possibility of con-sidering music and especially instruments which easily evade criticism by the idea of their fixity, as more than an embodiment of cultural knowledge parallel (though much different) to language. Their inter-textuality and lack of immunity to language is highlighted by the in-congruence of differing contexts which cannot be reconciled without the generality afforded by language. The prevalence or disappearance of certain performance venues are thus highly dependent on this func-tion of language which can manipulate meaning and change it. The fixity of instruments is of great use in doing so. Cultural memory is selective, not reflective, and is therefore very much constructed.

Both Racy and Qureshi are at heart basing their theses on the idea that an instrument has a position in society. With Racy, this is fairly clear, as the whole concept of a dialectic between adaptationism and idiosyncraticity assumes a singular position for the instrument. Qure-shi, however, may initially seem to have escaped this charge by her conception of a web of connotations. The multiplicity of connotations may easily be (mistakenly) confused with the multiplicity of positions. Yet for Qureshi, these connotations have developed around the in-strument over time. Through associations and discursive practices, the instrument has gathered around it a "web." This assumes a singular and unique position which may be understood in terms of multiple associations, but which is itself singular. It also assumes a singular "society" which may be culturally defined, although Qureshi acknowledges that within this society there are many nuances, such as generational differences and so on, which necessitate a consideration of the beholder. But the more important consequence of this singularity is that the context-sensitivity of the instrument is lost. Qureshi's understanding of meaning is thus limited to its "collection" and cannot account for its "release."

To help overcome some of these obstacles, I will present the following hypothesis. An instrument can best be understood through a "trialectic" between the capacities and limitations of its physicality (as explored by the materialist considerations of Racy), the context(s) in which the instrument generates meaning (and how it is related and influenced by other contexts), and the subject or beholder (whose historical interrelation with the instrument in its various guises and positions has to be understood and explored).[2] I rather suspect that the third of these factors, the history of the subject and his relation to other subjects, will be explored in greater depth as the impact of globalization is more strongly felt in the future. On the other hand, the preoccupation with materialist concerns has very much been the focus of organological studies in the past. Which leaves us with context, its capacity to generate meaning, and its relation with other contexts; a theme which will be explored through the study of the duduk which follows.

Notes

1. When I speak of language's context-independence, I of course mean this in a special way. Words, as linguistics has repeatedly and irrefutably demonstrated, are often context sensitive. However, we are taught that they are not. Common sense convinces us that a word denotes an object, thing, etc. and does so consistently and without error. We are thus able to subsume a great number of feelings and emotions under a word, such as "sadness," and thereby miss out on the nuances and differences, which in the absence of this word may well have caused us to forget the similarities and stress the differences between all those feelings which we know as "sadness."

2. Incidentally, this category also embraces the impact of discourse. What has been said about the instrument is very much part of the cultural history of the beholder.

Chapter 3

The Duduk

The word "duduk" seems to be derived from either the Turkish *düdük*, whistle (*Great Soviet Encyclopedia*, hereafter GSE, 1975, 8-438), or the Russian *duda*, pipe (Garlen; Gasparyan). The phonetic resemblance between the Turkish and Russian words is probably coincidental (Vasmer 1953, 378). The word and minor phonetic variants are used throughout Eastern Europe (Marcuse 1964, 157), Russia and the Caucasus (Atayan 1984, 615), but the name in much of the earlier literature is applied to various forms of the Turkish duct flute (Jacquot 1886, 76; Wright 1941, 58; Michel 1958, 1-673). Marcuse (1964, 158) is the only publication to define the duduk as a "conical oboe" while several Soviet encyclopedias later define the instrument in more detail also providing some information on its development in Armenia (Steinpress and Yampalski 1966, 167; GSE 1975, 8-438; Keldish 1974, 327). The *Musikalnaya Entsyklopedia* of 1974 states that "in the 1920s and `30s the Armenian duduk was improved by V. G. Buni, mostly retaining the nature [*typ*] of a folk instrument." The use of the name for both flute and cylindrical oboe is mentioned by several later publications (Picken 1975, 347; Atayan 1984, 615; Kazandjian 1984, 63; Baines 1992, 100; Ziegler 1994a, 1-847 and 1994b, 3-1278; Reinhard 1994, 9-1054), but what is clear from these sources is the degree to which the Soviet Union has long remained terra incognito for the Western scholar. This sometimes results in uncertainty as to the differences between duduk and düdük, in other words, the differences between a Turkish flute and an Armenian or Georgian oboe. In addition, the duduk is often referred to as an instrument of the Caucasus, an area that is home to over thirty nationalities.

It is important to realize that the duduk witnessed a unique development within Soviet Armenia, independent of the development of similar or related instruments in other parts of the Soviet Union, Turkey or Iran. In each of Armenia's neighboring countries, one may find an instrument constructionally very similar to the duduk. The *mey* of Turkey, the *balaban* of Iran, the *duduki* of Georgia, or the *yasti balaman* of Azerbaijan are all oboes with cylindrical bores. But their development has taken a different course resulting in notable differences in technique and sound quality.

The development of the duduk has been strongly patterned by sociopolitical events. Buni's reconstruction of the instrument, for example, has to some extent, instigated its appearance on the concert stage as a solo or ensemble instrument. The use of a diatonic scale and notation, has been a result of the Soviet policy of *Europeanization* (Levin 1980, 154; Djumaev 1993, 44). The playing of a number of duduks in unison instead of as a solo instrument with duduk drone and *dhol* (frame drum) accompaniment to dancing has arisen from its use in the folk ensemble, another Soviet establishment. Finally, the rise of Gasparyan on the international scene has coincided with Perestroika and Glasnost and the accompanying policies of allowing greater freedom for artists to establish reputations outside the Soviet Union. The resulting increase in popularity for the duduk has been fostered by a newfound freedom for musicians to choose their instruments and develop their skills on them, although in most cases, access to musical training in the Soviet sense is denied since it can no longer be afforded.

What has been of prime importance for the development of the duduk has been the strong and very much alive national feeling which led to one of the earliest demonstrations in the Soviet Union demanding independence (Snyder 1990, 16). Media for the communication of such feelings were increasingly sought since the relaxation of censorship in the Gorbachev era, contributing greatly to the redefinition of the already well-established symbolic capacities of the duduk. The arrangement and restructuring of the many meanings the variety of contexts briefly mentioned in the previous chapter brought about, were dependent on the salient potency of national identity, itself at once a product of, and influence on, cultural symbols and representative forms such as the duduk.

To understand the duduk's relation with Armenian nationalism in the twentieth century is a task related not so much to the country's pre-Soviet history, but to the perception of this history. The sheer and imposes itself in all realms of activity, among which music figures prominently. The conviction of this national history finds ready expression in the sounds of the duduk which fulfill not only the need to create symbols which endow the concept of such a history with substance, but allow the instrument to acquire a distinctive identity. The duduk is thus the consequence of the nation. Or perhaps, vice versa. At any rate, it shapes and forms the perception of a national history through the present, through the meanings it is able to generate today.

Chapter 4

Armenia—A Nation

In his encyclopedia of nationalism, Louis Snyder describes Armenian nationalism as "one of the most persistent mini-nationalisms in the world" (Snyder 1990, 16), resting a good deal of his article on the grounds that Armenia has survived centuries of foreign conquests including those of Persia, the Ottoman Empire, and Russia. He also cites a number of some 136 attacks claimed by the Armenian Secret Army against the Turks between 1975 and 1981 (ibid. 18), thus highlighting the extremism of which Armenian nationalism is capable.

Armenia is a small landlocked country bordering on the west with Turkey, on the north with Georgia, on the east with Azerbaijan, and on the south with Iran. It is the smallest of the Soviet bloc nations in size. The population today is estimated at 2.4 million, although the *Encyclopedia Britannica* states three million for 1997 (Britannica 1998, 545). The total number of Armenians around the world, including Western Armenians is around seven million, 750,000 (in 1990) of whom, live in the United States (Dudwick 1993, 265).

Nora Dudwick describes the politics of early Armenia as being the domain of "feuding dynastic principalities" (1993, 261). This, along with its location on the crossroads of Europe and Asia, has made it susceptible throughout the years to foreign invasion. Dudwick believes that it was this system that "ensured the survival of a distinct ethnic identity," although it is often argued that unity among Armenians depended in the earlier stages of Armenian history on a religious identity (Walker 1980, 12; Dudwick 1993, 263), a view which is supported by the three most important sources for our understanding of this early stage—Agathangelos, Khorenatsi and Elishe.[1] (Thomson

1982) Although, one of the earliest "heroes" of Armenian history, Vardan Mamigonian is said to have perished in a battle (in the fifth century A.D.) in order to resist the Persian Empire's "attempt to impose Zoroastrianism" (Garsoian 1997, 99-100), Elishe makes it clear that the battle was fought in order to keep Armenian traditional customs and way of life (Thomson, 1982). Considering the fact that Armenians had been identified as a people as much as a millennium earlier by Herodotus and Xenophon, this is hardly surprising.

Dudwick dates the roots of Armenian nationalism to the sixteenth century, "when an Armenian cultural renaissance began in the Diaspora"[2] (Dudwick 1994, 262). Suny on the other hand dates the formation of "national awareness" to the consolidation of Russian rule in (Eastern) Armenia in 1828 (Suny 1997, 115-116).

The difference between religious and national identity should not be overemphasized. Religious identity in Armenia is very much part of national identity. As Walker declares, "almost without exception Armenians are Christians, although often in a sociological rather than a religious sense" (Walker 1980, 12). Today the two events that have fueled, and continue to fuel nationalism most in Armenia are the 1915 genocide, and the Nagorno Karabagh conflict.

The 1915 Genocide

Beginning in 1894, Turkish nationalism under the Young Turks,[3] combined with other social and political factors, resulted in hatred towards and massacres of the Armenians. These massacres culminated in 1915 in what has often been described as "the first real genocide of the modern age." Boyadjian claims that the estimates for the number of Armenians killed vary between 800,000 and two million[4] (Boyadjian 1972, 1).

Both Dudwick and Walker agree that the memory of the genocide that took place in 1915 is of seminal importance for the strength of the Armenian identity. Dudwick claims that it has served "as a virtual 'charter of identity' even among families who had not directly experienced it" (Dudwick 1993, 265). Walker calls this crime which Armenians believe has gone unpunished and unrecognized, "the activating principle which unites almost all Armenians" (Walker, 1980, 13).

The Rise of Twentieth-Century Nationalism

The twentieth century saw changes in Armenia as well as the other "nations" and peoples that constituted the Soviet Union on an unprecedented magnitude. Modernization and industrialization made an impact in all spheres of life, although such developments were far from even and affected different parts of the USSR in different ways. A very useful way of viewing the rise of nationalism in the Soviet Union is provided for by Ernest Gellner's much acclaimed model. Gellner sees the rise of nationalism as a result of increased communications and the consequent melting pot effect. Only instead of one single melting pot, we have a number of them, determined by a number of already existing factors and the inconsistent capacities of assimilation in different places. Gellner's thesis is based on the assumption that "culture" is, more or less, the ground of all nations:

> Cultural nuances in the agrarian world are legion: they are like raindrops in a storm, there is no counting of them. But when they all fall on the ground, they do not, as it were, coagulate into one large all-embracing puddle, nor do they remain separate: in fact, they aggregate into a number of distinct, large, often mutually hostile puddles. The aggregation, the elimination of plurality and nuance anticipated by the internationalists, does indeed take place, but it leaves behind not one large universal culture-puddle, but a whole set of them (1997, 33).

In Armenia, a number of factors contributed to the formation of a national attitude. The unification and homogenization of culture, which was necessary for making the 1915 genocide a cultural memory able to provide nationalism with impetus, was a result of diverse factors.

Soon after the formation of the USSR, a policy known as *korenizatsia* was established to allow the peripheral republics their supposed "right of self-determination." Korenizatsia was the policy of nativization, and seems quite obviously to contradict Marxist ideology. It is in fact a point of digression from Marxism and demonstrates Lenin's awareness of nationalism's potency.

For a number of reasons, including the need for support for the new regime from a large number of republics and the ideological centrality in Leninist thought, of making "all nations equal," the more "backward" republics were subjected to major changes and advances to allow them to equal the more "advanced" republics. It was hoped that in this way, national inequality would finally disappear, removing nationalism from the Soviet social sphere. Korenizatsia allowed nations to retain and develop their language and culture, including music. Folk music collecting and arranging formed a major part of this process.

The Stalinist years saw a reversal of the process, but korenizatsia never really lost its strength in the seven decades of Soviet rule. Its institutions remained. By the 1960s Khrushchev was in a position to effect a federalization that allowed the development of local power to an unprecedented degree.

Korenizatsia drew on the resources offered by the latest media of dissemination, most notably, the radio. Through radio, cultural representative forms such as music were standardized in the same way that the spread of publishing helped standardize language. A "national" music (*azkain yerajshdoutioun*) was created. Culture, in all its guises, underwent a homogenization that allowed Armenians to speak of their culture.

An awareness of culture as the basis of nation developed as contact with other nations in the Soviet Union and outside increased. The idea of culture found unchallenged support in *azkain* (translated as both "folk" and "national") music and art. This "construction of self" was influenced greatly by other nations' use of such notions of "culture," and explain the similarity in the development of such culturally representative forms as "folk ensemble music."

Unsurprisingly, the inequalities, cultural and otherwise, of the numerous peoples of the Soviet Union were never really bridged. Their contact and awareness of each other, on the other hand, had increased immensely. It was not long before unequal access to resources was perceived and nations' relative deprivations were transformed to "mutually hostile puddles." The time of the completed assimilation of the immensely diverse cultures of the USSR, the Soviet man, never arrived. Nationalism, however, did.

The Nagorno Karabagh Conflict

This conflict which is one of many consequences of the problems inherited by post-Soviet national feeling, began in 1988, when "the largest nationalist demonstration in the seventy-year history of the Soviet Union" took place, with the purpose of demanding that the Nagorno Karabagh Autonomous Region be incorporated into Armenia (Snyder, 1990, 16).

The causes of this conflict stretch back to a brief period of Armenian independence between 1918 and 1920, which ended when Armenia fell under Soviet power. Although populated principally by Armenians, the region of Nagorno Karabagh was placed inside the territory and administration of Soviet Azerbaijan. With *glasnost*, the demand for the transfer of this region to Armenian control became possible and resulted in the onset of violence in Sumgait (near Baku), Kirovabad, and Baku between 1988 and 1990.

The passion hitherto directed against the Turks was to a degree transferred against the Azeris, who are essentially thought of in Armenia, as a Turkish people. Croissant calls the separation of Karabagh from Armenia "a gaping wound in the Armenian national consciousness" (1998, 139). Although some have pointed out religious differences among the causes of this conflict (Potschiwalow and Schostakowsky 1996, 130), most scholars seem to agree that "ethnic nationalism" is the most central motivating force (Chorbajian et al. 1994, 49-50).[5]

Notes

1. These sources are important because "the image of the past as expounded by these classical authors has had a profound impact in the last two centuries on the way in which Armenians look upon themselves, their history, and their nation" (Thomson 1982, 2).

2. "The creation of diasporas throughout Armenian history has been the consequence of destabilizing forces that have affected the homeland since early times. These forces have ranged from economic crises and deprivation, to political instability, conquest, religious persecution, massacre, and deportation." And "Between the fourth century A.D. and the massacres of 1915 and 1922, successive waves of Armenian immigrants and refugees established hundreds of expatriate communities in over thirty different lands throughout the world" (Dekmejian 1997, 413).

3. The *Oxford English Dictionary* refers to the Young Turks as "Ottomans of the turn of the century who tried to rejuvenate the Turkish Empire and bring it more into line with European ideas" (OED 1989, XVIII-689).

4. Snyder estimates between 800,000 and a million deaths in total (1990, 17). Dadrian estimates over a million deaths during World War I alone (1995, XVIII).

5. Joffé points out four main influences in the region, three of which apply to the Armenia-Azerbaijan conflict: nationalism, territorial claims, and Islam (1996, 17).

Part 2

The Centrality of National Identity
to Perceptions of the Duduk

Having established the shocking capacity of nationalism in the twentieth century in Armenia and noting its reliance on the emergence of a core envisaging of national culture, I will focus now on how the duduk contributed in the construction of forms of representation of this culture. An instrument's ability to combine its stable and reliable "fixity" with an aesthetically grounded "affect" that depends on its elusive nature for its potency is what gives the duduk unchallenged capacity for providing identities with the tools for self assertion and construction. Fixity raises the credibility of historical constructions of place using the duduk, while the elusiveness of affect allows it to be maneuvered as required for the construction of identity.

Chapter 5

The History of the Development of the Duduk

Armenia had been under Russian dominion for almost a century prior to the onset of Soviet rule. Russian influence and the dissemination of late-nineteenth century Romanticism affected urban areas in Armenia where Western-style composition incorporated traditional Armenian folk tunes in an attempt to propagate Armenian national culture. Similar movements appeared throughout Europe. The earliest duduk recordings I have been able to find are from urban areas, where musical development had taken place independently of rural areas. Despite an interest in the collecting of folk songs, which characterized the last two decades of the nineteenth century (GSE 1975, 2-353), I have found no material on the duduk as played in rural areas in a predominantly rural Armenia. It seems to me highly likely that in sound quality and playing technique, the rural duduk of this period closely resembled the mey of Eastern Turkey, a region then inhabited by a large number of Armenians. Despite this lack of information, duduk playing today seems to be moving in the direction of what is perceived as pre-Soviet patterns. The extent to which this tradition has been "invented" in the Hobsbawmian sense of the word must for the moment remain a matter for speculation.

The 1920s and '30s

The early history of the duduk was summed up by Gasparyan as follows:

> First the duduk was nothing more than a reed (*ghamish*). Not the reed that we have today, but a longer reed which formed the whole duduk. Over the years, the size of the reed grew smaller, and an extra part (*mas*) was added at the end.

According to Gasparyan, the duduk is "fifteen-hundred years old." An "introduction to the duduk" found in an advertisement of one of Gasparyan's CDs claims that "Western scholars trace its existence back fifteen-hundred years though Soviet Armenian musicologists have found evidence dating the instrument as far back as 1200 B.C." (also Schnabel 1998, 54). Garlen said that "some people claim that the instrument was known in 3500 B.C., but for me, not every piece of wood with a hole in it is a duduk."[1] I have been unable to ascertain what evidence such claims are based upon, however it seems very likely that cylindrical oboes with similar construction to the duduk have been played in the Caucasus for many centuries.

The onset of the Soviet period provides us with more solid grounds for understanding the development of the instrument. This period, beginning for Armenia in 1921, brought about some major changes in the lives of folk musicians including the new context of the "folk ensemble," as well as a new Westernized system of education. In order to understand fully the nature and extent of these changes, it is necessary to consider Soviet culture policy in the satellite nations in the 1920s and '30s, as well as social forces partly dependent but not derived from "above."

We may classify the aims of Soviet ideology in three rough categories. Firstly, the goal of "advancement," which took on the particular form of Europeanization. Secondly, the elimination of any cultural forms suggestive of class differences, such as opera. Thirdly the survival of "national" elements in culture. The factors emanating from "below" on the other hand seem to coagulate around the workings of national identity. It is partly through this dialectic that, in light of the considerations mentioned in chapter 4, the rise of a folk ensemble can be explained, a folk ensemble playing "national" folk music, but playing it "in a Western way."

Europeanization[2]

Djumaev has described the 1920s to mid-1930s in the Soviet Union as a period of "open polemics between different cultural forces." In particular, these concerned the inherent contradictions between the traditional musics of the various satellite states and the music of contemporary European-style composers (Djumaev 1993, 43). The assimilation of so-called "European professional music" was a priority of Soviet culture policy (and remained so until the collapse of the Soviet Union) presumably as it was generally believed to be the only true means of advancement.

Levin believes that the adoption of the Russian language and European art forms, which were to be a means of cultural advancement (a favorite word of the Soviet authorities), formed "one of the founding postulates" of Leninism. In Armenia, the learning of the Russian language was made obligatory at secondary schools only in 1938 (Matossian 1975, 154), as a result of Stalin's temporary reversal of korenizatsia. (I should note here that the country had been under Russian rule since 1828, and had seen a greater number of "advancements" since then.)[3] The adoption of European art forms on the other hand was already under way in Armenia in the second half of the nineteenth century evidenced by the creation of a new school in musical composition, several professional music companies, and European style musical ensembles (GSE 1975, 2-353). A number of Armenian composers also employed European compositional techniques in their works during this period (Atayan 1980, 19-334, 335; GSE 1975, 2-353).

As Levin points out, "Soviet-style Marxism-Leninism took it on principle that it was the business of government to serve as an arbiter of cultural values and artistic taste." It was considered that state institutionalization of all the arts was necessary if cultural policy was to succeed. In fact, the two could not be separated at all. Lenin's view of art, according to Lukin, was such that although he considered it "a specific form of aesthetic cognition and activity," its central function could be transformed to a political tool through a unification of artistic creativity and the social proletariat movement (Lukin 1976, 178). So art must serve the purpose of the state. Djumaev considers state institutionalization as the "first tendency of cultural policy concerning traditional music." In Armenia along with the ensemble of national folk instruments set up in 1926, there was the establishment of the Komitas Conservatory in 1923, the Philharmonic Society in 1932, the

Spendiarov Academic Theatre of Opera and Ballet in 1933, the Composers' Union of Armenia—also in 1933, the Estrada (variety stage) Orchestra in 1938, and the Paronian Theatre of Musical Comedy in 1942.

In speaking of the effects of Europeanization, Levin refers to the "idolization of European masterpieces" that typified the training of young ethnic music performers (Levin 1980, 154). The result was "ethnic" music, which was presented in a European manner. Musicians had to adapt not only their playing, but all realms of musical activity to European models. Discourse was not excluded.

It is difficult to say with any accuracy exactly when the widespread use of terms such as "melisma" (*melism*) and "temperament" (pronounced as in German) began to be used by duduk players. Such terms are commonly found in conversations with Arsen, who is in his thirties, and to a lesser degree in the musical discourse of older players. The 1938 policy of making Russian obligatory in secondary schools never really foregrounded the language, and few people spoke it well. As a result, Armenian remained very much the language spoken in the ethnically homogeneous Armenia (Matossian 1975, 154). The use of Western musical terms among duduk players, therefore, must have developed relatively recently as the duduk has been taught at the conservatory only since 1978.[4]

Elimination of Cultural Forms
Suggestive of Class Differences

C. Prudian, professor of Armenian music at the conservatory of Yerevan, informed me that for several years after 1920 an attempt was made to "remove" Western-style classical music completely. Although this experiment only lasted a few years, the word "classical" was replaced by "professional." Similarly, for the case of Uzbekistan, Levin speaks of "the supposition of a gradual evolution of musical substance from its spontaneous generation in the pristine state of "folk creativity" to that more subtle and complex condition which in the Soviet lexicon is subsumed under the rubric "professional" (rather than "classical") music" (Levin 1980, 151). In other words, "professional music" was perceived as a more "advanced" form of folk music, where the association with social standing, or class, was transferred to the notion of folk and professional as different stages of development of the same music. This was seen as a solution in the attempt to eliminate the idea of the folk-classical dichotomy. Levin lists the radio ensembles, performing troupes, recording artists, amateur groups, and the educational system, from conservatories down to musical elementary schools, as groups which were "organized around the principle of maintaining a high level of visibility for *natsionalnaya muzika*, so that in each republic it exists at least on a par with *klassicheskaya muzika*: Western music," classical music being of course, the music of "the bourgeois countries" (Levin 1980, 153).

The Survival of *Natsionalnaya Muzika* (National Music)

Levin points out an important distinction between "*natsionalizm* which carries the perfidious connotation of 'separatism,' and *natsionalnaya politika*, nationalities policy—the principle of integration and cooperation between nationalities, founded on Lenin's original vision of national-cultural autonomy within a world socialist system" (Levin 1980, 152). Although it is generally agreed by scholars that Marx did not take the issue of nationalism at all seriously in his writings, for the most part ignoring it on the basis that real differences are not differences of nationality but differences in class, Lenin, placed in a different temporal milieu, was quick to realize the importance of nationalism as a force to be reckoned with. Indeed in Armenia, the already mentioned term *azkain* denotes "national" as well as "folk" music, and carries the connotation of "professional." Djumaev speaks of the "general line of politics" that "never completely prohibited nor eradicated traditional music." The main goal was to cleanse traditional music (i.e. to Europeanize it), not to forbid it. One method of cleansing was European-style harmonization, to which, one might speculate, Armenian musicians would not have readily adapted, considering the essentially monodic nature of Armenian traditional music.

Among the means employed to effect these changes and impose these policies, was the reconstruction of traditional instruments.[5] As we know from Keldish, the "work" carried out on the duduk to "improve" it was undertaken by a certain V. G. Buni (Keldish 1974, 327). A standardization of three types of duduks must have taken place, with a significant "innovation" being the introduction of the lower register duduk—called the *Bunifon*. The use of the term "Bunifon" seems to suggest that the pre-Soviet duduk may have been an instrument similar to the zurna, in that it must have been closer to it in terms of register, for if the lower register was not the most significant innovation made by Buni, why did it receive his name? Unfortunately, my limitations in terms of information on the Bunifon impede a more thorough portrayal of its usage and context. The exceptionally low register of the duduk used in the 78rpm recording [ref. no. ICS0020821 (1)] available at the British Library suggests that it may be a Bunifon. The duduk playing in this recording is mostly in unison with a baritone singer, whose range far exceeds that of the Bunifon, forcing changes of octaves on the latter throughout the piece. The slow introduction to the piece is a duduk solo closely resembling the "sad song genre" of today. In addition, ornamentation, vibrati, and use of indefinite pitch (subsumed today under the general category of *melism*) provide evidence that the present-day conception of "traditional duduk music" is not entirely "invented."

There are three 78rpm recordings of duduk music at the National Sound Archives in London, which must have been recorded in this period, as 78s were not in use much later than the end of the '30s. These include five pieces played by duduks and one played by zurnas. All the recordings were made in Tiflis, by Armenian duduk (and zurna) players. In all cases, the use of a more or less diatonic Western scale is clear, although the use of vibrati and ornaments is far from limited, especially in the slow sections which exhibit the quality of sadness which is so intensely portrayed today. The sound is never as strident as is the zurna's, and it is difficult to tell whether circular breathing is employed (by the melody player) as it clearly is on the zurna recording.

Thus, Soviet policy may be held responsible for "advancing" the duduk by endowing it with what was perceived as a more sophisticated sound and reconstructing it to allow duduk technique to "develop." The case of the duduk is an apt metonym for a much larger process of advancing folk culture.

Having said all this, I should add that I find the persistent emphasis and reliance on government actions to explain the development of such cultural phenomena in the Soviet Union (common among scholars) somewhat one-sided. The policy of Europeanization was indeed the work of government, but its widespread acceptance must be interpreted also from a government-peoples relationship perspective. People's cooperation is often more necessary than is believed. The case of Turkey in the same period as that under discussion illustrates my point. When the government controlled radio in an attempt to disseminate "authentic Turkish tunes," people ended up switching off their radios or tuning their sets to receive Egyptian broadcasts (Stokes 1992).

The public acceptance of Europeanization may be understood through a consideration of national identity. Scholars in general agree that the years of Soviet ascendancy up until the end of Stalin's rule were, in terms of nationalism, dormant. In contrast, the need to express and fulfill this identity must certainly have been alive judging from the sudden emergence of extreme nationalist activity as soon as a slight leniency on the part of the Soviet government allowed it. The presence of "other," which, at least in the urban population, had persisted, activated the need for a construction of self in contradistinction to these "others." The forms of such cultural expression were thus copied from Russians and Europeans, although the substance was clearly perceived as different and distinctive. This distinctive nature of "copied" European forms and norms endowed with authentic Armenian folk creations, allowed it to be conceived as an embodiment and representative of national culture. To ignore the role of nongovernment agencies in the continued production of forms of Europeanized "national" folk culture is to ignore the fact that this very production (on a far smaller scale and in a different guise of course) enjoyed its acme at the height of Armenian nationalism in the third quarter of the nineteenth century.

To summarize, then, this period was seemingly marked by significant changes in all aspects of duduk players' lives. It was only decades later, however, that most players began to adapt to these requirements, since the new policies could only be implemented by introducing a sufficient number of regional ensembles and educational institutions. Although the first folk ensemble was set up as early as 1926, it is unlikely that the effects of Europeanization on duduk players were widespread, since:

1. there was only one folk ensemble in Yerevan during this period,
2. there were no *technicums* until much later, and as already mentioned, the conservatory did not begin teaching the duduk until 1978, and
3. the population of Armenia at this time was still mostly rural, and it is unlikely that these policies would have affected the majority of duduk players due to restricted communications.

The Margaryan Era

Djivan Gasparyan related to me the following story of how he became interested in the duduk as a small boy.

> My parents had taken me to the movies. In those days the movies were silent, and the music played was live. A number of duduk players sat in the front row and watching the movie, played along. They knew where to start and when to stop, because I'm sure they had seen the movie many times. I don't remember what the movie was like, but I can certainly remember the music. After it was over, I went up to the players and asked them if I can have lessons. Well, one of them told me, you are too young, and besides you must buy a duduk. How are you going to afford it? I asked them whether they would give me lessons if I had a duduk, and they said yes. So for the next month, I would save up money by collecting bottles for which the owner of a restaurant who knew me would pay. Eventually when I had collected enough I went back to the players, who were so surprised by my devotion that they said such a boy could not fail to become a great duduk player. So I was given free lessons.

Gasparyan's story marks the beginning of a new period in duduk history, characterized by the rise of Margar Margaryan, who made the duduk known to a wider audience, and redefined its position which had hitherto been viewed as that of an instrument "played by shepherds to pass the time." This rise in status, and growth in popularity in urban areas must have, to some extent, been catalyzed by the establishment of the "House of Broadcasting and Sound Recording" in 1938, and the "House of People's Arts" which was first set up in 1936, and of which there were some 175 by 1970 throughout the Soviet Union. The function of the former is clear from its name, but the latter's purpose is only roughly defined in the *Great Soviet Encyclopedia* as "providing organizational, methodological, and artistic guidance to amateur artists in state club institutions (palaces and houses of culture, clubs, and parks of culture and recreation)." At any rate, the promotion of knowledge about traditional music was furthered and helped the provision of Western-style musical education to an increasing number of people (GSE 1975, 8-530). These establishments came at a time when, despite the highly inefficient use of confiscated land, people were continually being moved to urban areas.

Growing urbanization and the rise of folk ensembles moved the duduk from its rural venues where it was treated more like the *zurna*

(shawm), to a place within the folk ensembles. A folk ensemble conductor explained to me that "having four duduks in the orchestra is a
relatively recent thing" and that during the forties and fifties, there
were in fact two duduks per ensemble which may have required special attention on the part of composers, since the sound of the duduk is
very soft and may easily be drowned by the other instruments. It
seems likely that this pattern of playing several duduks together in
folk ensembles ensured its use as a member of all-duduk ensembles,
which performed in the front rows of cinemas as Gasparyan describes.

The professionalization of duduk playing was accompanied by
the need and will to adapt to Western concepts of music. Although we
cannot say for certain when the use of the diatonic scale was standardized, the importance of notation had manifested itself to such a degree
that well-known players were obliged to learn. Vahan tells me that it
was his teacher—Vatche Hovsepian, who taught notation to Margar
Margaryan (who became well known only in the forties), and this in
the late fifties, many years after achieving fame. At its outset the folk
ensemble did not require its members to read notation—a condition
which would have been highly limiting—but with growing institutionalization and an increase in the number of players whose musical education included notation, this pattern was slowly replaced by the new
requisites for Westernized training. With the growing number of folk
ensembles, the prestige of playing in one lost some of its momentum,
and Margaryan and his contemporaries' inability to read notation must
have affected their image as role models. The growing status of notation thus ousted "playing by ear" but it is very likely that the fame of
Margaryan and some of his contemporaries was partly established
through their status as members of a folk ensemble.[6]

One of Margaryan's contemporaries, Levon Madoyan, is the soloist in two pieces from the LPs found at the British Library (reference
numbers MF321 and MF303). In the first we have a slow sad song
played by two duduks, the second acting as drone, until the dhol
(drum) enters and the piece transforms into a kind of slow dance. Vibrato is used throughout the piece in the sad song section and one
hardly ever hears the nasal sound that is more prominent in the earlier
recordings. As the tempo picks up, and the presence of the dhol is felt,
the sound becomes increasingly nasal and zurna-like. An interesting
element of the playing is the use of a pianissimo in rendering a repeated passage, seemingly in order to provide a contrast. Although the
date of this recording is not known, the LP format and Madoyan's
presence suggest the 1950s.

The second is a sort of duduk concerto, where Madoyan is accompanied by the Aram Merangulian Ensemble. The orchestration, the entry of the duduk and the overall shape of the piece betray a very strongly Western classical influence. The orchestration carefully avoids any danger of the duduk sound being drowned, and the character of the piece is beyond doubt best described by the word "sad." A small footnote describes the story of the song: "A charming and simple melody played on the duduk. The song expresses the boy's love and longing for his mother. He hears her sweet voice, he feels her warm kiss, but alas! It is only a dream."

The fact that the duduk was already considered an instrument worthy of being treated as a solo instrument in a mini-concerto environment, is evidence of its urbanization, or more precisely, its growing popularity in urban areas. This, together with the increasing use of notation, acted as yet another stabilizer of cultural form as embodied in the duduk, or to paraphrase, it was a medium of standardization of cultural memory, which, following Gellner's perspective assisted in the homogenization of culture on which concepts of nation are based.

Vatche Hovsepian and After
(1960s to the End of Soviet Rule)

Opinions differ as to whether some of the famous duduk players are worthy of their fame, however, there is an overall agreement that Vatche Hovsepian was the "greatest of all duduk players." Unlike his predecessors, Hovsepian had an international reputation (although to a far lesser degree than Gasparyan). A duduk player's book describes his performance in Iceland where "not a single Armenian lives," as so successful that encores were demanded several times. Gasparyan speaks of two schools of duduk playing:

> Those who follow Hovsepian's methods belong to the Hovsepian school. They concentrate on technique, they play a more generally Eastern repertoire, or rather they are more Caucasian, but not specifically Armenian, whereas my school concentrates on creating Armenian sounds, and technique is not so important for us. I always tell my students that the most important thing about the duduk is its sound.

It was in the sixties that nationalist feeling first manifested itself visibly in Armenia during the Soviet period. The fiftieth anniversary of the Turkish massacres in 1965 was accompanied by violence (Suny 1997, 376; Matossian 1975, 158), and although nationalist attitudes had remained the same since the twenties, a growth in the number of events which gave them expression defined the path which ensuing forms of nationalism were to take. It is during this period that the symbolic status of the duduk seems to have been elevated, heightening the value of its association with the Armenian nation to the degree that it reached in 1989, when Brian Eno presented it on the international scene as a "representation" of Armenia.

According to Vahan, the duduk was used on a number of occasions in nationalist demonstrations. One particular event was a demonstration in 1978, which took the form of traditional dances, in traditional costume in Yerevan's central square, in which, whenever possible, the dancers faced Mount Ararat, another symbol of national identity. The dancers were accompanied by traditional instruments, among them, the duduk.[7]

The growing international status of the duduk, which culminated in 1989, also fostered the strength of its association with Armenia. Hovsepian was already performing outside the Soviet Union in the 1950s while Gasparyan was first heard in America in 1959. The duduk's access to the international community however was limited. According to Gasparyan:

> In the old days, the [invitations to play in Europe or America] had to be approved by the central committee from Moscow, I would have an invitation from France, but they would have to go through the Politburo and wait ten or fifteen days to find out if they get the approval. Nowadays, I get the letter right away.(Woodard 1999)

Gasparyan's growing popularity first received official recognition when he was made "People's Artist of Armenia" in 1973. By 1978, the duduk's status had grown enough for it to be considered a principle instrument for study at the conservatory. Hitherto duduk study had only been possible at Technicums where it was taught as part of a wind player's course.

Gasparyan's style has certainly been the most influential element in the development of duduk technique since the 1970s. Dezirgenian, Gasparyan's recording engineer, describes Djivan's innovations on the duduk: "He took from the popular style, which was kind of primitive and elemental compared to what he plays now. He added half-notes that kind of spiced and made it more flavorful, and people loved this, because it came closer to the heart" (Wald 1999). The "spicy half-

notes" and other ornaments which "made it more flavourful" are certainly present in all the early recordings of the duduk I have heard.
The great number of Europeanized compositions, however, which
made use of folk themes, had greatly reduced the number of ornaments, slides, and melismata which were previously such an integral
part of duduk technique, making Gasparyan's "return" to these more
"Armenian" elements very welcome. Although we do not know to
what degree such elements were really pre-Soviet (they are not found
in the mey recordings), today they serve as a bastion of the "age-old
Armenian tradition." It is perhaps charmingly ironic that the effects of
Soviet "advancement" should be referred to as "primitive" and "elemental."

The Post-Soviet Decade

As access to the international world music stage improved, Gasparyan came more and more to represent Armenia in his many concerts and recordings abroad. "Whenever I go somewhere, Armenia is
proud, because I'm representing the country in the best way possible."
Woodard calls him "musical ambassador of Armenia." As a representative of Armenian culture, it is felt that Gasparyan has brought to the
fore the sadness characteristic of the duduk, employing this element as
a means of identification with years of oppressive foreign rule which
has made sadness an integral part of the perceived nature of an Armenian.[8]

The proliferation of recordings of duduk music, in and outside
Armenia, has resulted in an analogous increase in the number of players. The great popularity of the instrument throughout Armenia has
brought about previously unknown events and ensembles. Among the
former, noteworthy are the two recent duduk competitions (1998
1999), and among the latter, Gasparyan's fifty-member duduk ensemble (composed of his former and current students), which has performed in numerous concerts throughout the former Soviet Union.

Another notable result of Gasparyan's international reputation
has been the duduk's rising status. Gasparyan's four UNESCO prizes,
over fifty recordings (his own estimate), and "ambassadorship" have
effected a change in the long-held associations of the duduk with village life. According to Dezirgenian, "Only a few years ago, the duduk
was for shepherds in the villages; now it is in cities and mainstream

cultural centers, with three-piece-suit people rather than just villagers" (Wald 1999).

The "Armenianness" of the duduk has been one of its greatest attractions, but as Gasparyan continues collaborating in projects which are far from purely Armenian, such as the latest album "Black Rock" in which he plays in ensemble with Canadian guitarist Michael Brook, the duduk world is likely to find models to imitate in the array of syncretic styles that its greatest proponent has advocated.[9]

> He has adapted the instrument to fit Western melodies, and you can hear the metamorphosis or the mixture of the cultures. But he's hoping that from now on there will be more accompanying or being in the domain of the traditional music rather than East-West collaboration or mixture. Because the thing that duduk loves is improvisation. When you put duduk in limitations, in cues and stuff, it becomes just another instrument in the orchestra (Dezirgenian in Wald 1999).

Whether considering Gasparyan's recordings with the Kronos Quartet, the Los Angeles Philharmonic, or Michael Brook, the movement away from the Soviet-period solo playing (which was heavily influenced by Western classical elements and limited in ornamentation and freedom, as pointed out earlier) is clearly observed, while on the other hand his solo recordings have attempted to convey his devotion to the perceived traditionally Armenian elements of duduk music.

From conversations with certain duduk players, it became apparent to me that Gasparyan's enormous popularity and inordinately far-reaching power in all matters concerning the duduk had provided grounds for a not small number of people to criticize his playing and derogate his supposed greatness. The growth of this tendency is fostering the idea that Hovsepian was the undisputed "greatest" performer on the duduk, a belief which may in future found a different path as a new role model is sought after Gasparyan.

The future development of the duduk may continue to be determined by the development of national identity in Armenia. Increasing Western attention and efforts to Westernize the Caucasus, as well as the possibility of a Transcaucasian economic union, will develop Armenia's communications with its neighbors. The prospects of oil in Baku and the building of a pipeline through Armenia will in all likelihood increase foreign attention in coming years. National identity which is highly dependent on well-defined cultural demarcators, will in the growth of communications in the region require new symbols, and depend on the adaptability of existing ones. The duduk's discerned uniqueness may be manipulated to serve such needs.

The history of the duduk, then, is the history of a cultural homogenization which parallels and is defined by the emergence of the Armenian nation as concept and as ground for nationalist activity. The relation between duduk and national identity is far more than a web of associations embodied in the former. The two have been interdependent and have provided impetus for mutual development.

Notes

1. This last date no doubt refers to findings of the first nay in Ancient Egypt (the "nay" being, according to Garlen, "the name of the duduk before it acquired its current name from the Russian 'dudka'") in the fourth millenium B.C. Although double reeds were not found with the nay, it is very possible that they could be fitted on one. Manniche claims that in appearance the oboes and nay are very similar at the proximal end. We know that reeds could be placed not only inside the main body, but also so as to surround the body at its proximal end. In addition, it is well known that ancient oboes have been found throughout Asia (Manniche 1975).

2. The use of this word I have adopted from Levin. "I use the term 'Europeanization' rather than 'Westernization' or 'Modernization' because it was specifically European models that Soviet ideologues had in mind as they planned the cultural future of Central Asia" (Levin 1993, 52).

3. It is a subject very much open to debate, whether the "cultural development" of Armenia was more significant during Russian rule than it was during the Soviet period. It is, however, important to note that the latter changes affected a far larger segment of the population than did the former. The Soviets urbanized Armenia, presenting a cultural development which penetrated a far more variegated population than hitherto.

4. In Armenia there are musical schools which are attended while students are at primary or secondary schools, *technicums* and conservatories. Technicums are mainly for those who have been unable to attend music schools and have decided after school to get a musical education (often to be accepted to play in a folk ensemble). Conservatories provide the highest level of musical training and education and are the most prestigious. The main difference between the two is that while the former aims at an all-round education, whereby students are expected to play a number of instruments, the conservatory expects a higher level of ability on a single instrument.

5. The word "reconstruction" is used by both Djumaev and Levin in reference to the specific process of "innovating" that took place throughout the Soviet Union in the 1920s and '30s. It should not be confused with the use of the word to designate imitations of early instruments (such as those used in

the Baroque period). The "re-" here does not imply constructing in exactly the same way as previously, but constructing in a new and supposedly improved way.

6. See also Rice (1994, 148-50).

7. This incident is also mentioned by Snyder (1990, 17-18).

8. Whether considering the Mongol, Persian, Ottoman or Russian invasions, Armenians have been forced to regard foreign rule as oppressive throughout history.

9. Despite the phonetic horrors of this word, it is used in the literature on Armenia, and I find it indispensable for the expression of the closeness of the duduk's association with the nation. Many apologies.

Chapter 6

The Duduk as
Cultural Demarcator

To form an overview of the duduk's position and its separability from similar instruments in neighboring regions, it may prove enlightening to take a closer look at the two instruments most compared with it, the *balaban* of northwest Iran, and the *mey* of Turkey.

From Albright's description of the balaban in the *Encyclopedia Iranica*, we know that it is 35 cm long and has seven fingerholes and a thumbhole, made of mulberry or walnut, with a bore diameter of 1.5 cm, and a double reed 6 cm long (Albright 1989, 3-569). Of the balaban's playing technique we know little. Albright mentions the use of circular breathing. Of its performance context we know through Blum, that it is used to accompany dancing, but that it is also played solo (Blum 1980, 9-306). In *Grove's Dictionary of Musical Instruments*, there is mention of its use with the *chogur* (lute) and *qaval* (frame drum) to accompany singing of an *asheq*. Its sound is described as having a "warm, full tone" (During et al. 1984, 1-113).

The constructional similarities between duduk and balaban are striking, but a consideration of Wanda Bryant's study of ninety-one double reed instruments of which thirty-four have cylindrical bores questions the validity of basing a comparison on major constructional features (Bryant 1990, 132-176). On the other hand, the duduk has eight, not seven fingerholes, and an additional tuning hole on the posterior side, which is missing on the balaban. The reed of the balaban is almost half the length of the duduk's, and the two instruments are made of different woods. As for technique, the little we know does not allow a comparison. However, circular breathing is used on the duduk only in dances, which does not currently form a prominent part of its repertoire (circular breathing is always used by the drone player). Further, I have never come across a duduk-lute-singer ensemble.

A closer comparison is possible with the mey thanks to Picken's comprehensive account (Picken 1975, 475-81). Picken observed that a balaban that he examined was identical to the Turkish mey "reported so far in Artvin, Erzurum, Guemuesane, Kars and Mus" (ibid. 480). He also states that the terms "mey" or "nay" are used "exclusively for a cylindrical, turned, wooden pipe, sometimes with a slightly tapering bore, with seven fingerholes and a thumbhole, excited by a very large, elongate, bilamellate, concussion reed . . . and made for preference from walnut or apricot wood." He then gives further constructional details which in one of the three standard sizes in which the mey is found closely resemble that of the duduk (ibid. 475-476).

The number of fingerholes which Picken states to be "generally seven," is the greatest perceivable difference. Picken quotes Saygun as having reported a form "from Kars with eight fingerholes, the lowest of which is never covered." On the duduk, the eighth hole is certainly used, but requires more forceful blowing than when a lesser number of holes are stopped. Another difference is that the reed is not always inserted directly into the body of the instrument, but into an adapter called the ölcü. (ibid. 476)

One important difference where playing technique is concerned is that on the mey the fingerholes are not invariably constant in diameter. The invariability of the shape and size of fingerholes is of prime importance to the duduk, where covering holes to different degrees is very central not only to pitch, but to the sound created, since any compromises offered by lipping are avoided in favor of better and more consistent sound quality. It is difficult to say how much a duduk player would be affected by an inconsistency in fingerhole diameter.

On the mey, the distance between fingerholes is constant, whereas on the duduk, it is not. Garlen knew all the distances on all the different types of duduks by memory, and the relationships between distances are strictly adhered to when making a duduk of unusual type upon request.

There can be little doubt that it is the differences in playing technique that are essentially responsible for the overall difference in sound quality, which seems considerable. Picken states that "in playing the mey the fingerholes are stopped with the palmar surface of the terminal phalanges" (ibid. 477). From this we must assume that a different method is used for partial closures, to that which is used on the duduk (see appendix B: duduk technique). To be sure, partial closures are commonly used on the mey—"by half covering certain fingerholes (not by cross fingering) a single, fully chromatic octave can be obtained" (ibid. 478). In blowing, too, major differences are noted. Circular breathing, Picken points out, is as important to the *meyci* as to the *zurnaci*.[1] Another difference in technique is the vibrato. On the mey, "the player may shake the instrument with both hands, so as to generate a vibrato" (ibid. 477), whereas on the duduk, it is the lower jaw which is shaken to create the same effect.

The range utilized on most mey is one octave, although the instrument from Kars (with the eight fingerholes) is capable of a tenth. Its "natural scale is a major scale." The duduk is capable of an eleventh, and one can hardly speak of its "natural scale" (see appendix B), since lipping is so prominently used to adjust pitch.

Picken speaks of the mey (in much the same manner as the zurna) as providing ritornelli for a singer—with a *davul* (ibid. 478). The 78 rpm recordings of duduk trios are evidence of the fact that before the 1950s this description may have applied to the duduk. Such similarities between mey and balaban bring to light the "uniqueness" of the development of the duduk in the last fifty years, a development which has been highly dependent on the growth and development of the duduk's role as cultural and social demarcator. New directions, which broaden the gap between duduk and instruments of a similar nature from neighboring regions, may be actively sought if in the future contact with these neighboring peoples is improved.[2]

I hope to have shown that although the similarities between the duduk and closely related instruments are not to be overlooked, one cannot, as David Brown has done in "Basic Info for Mey or Duduk,"[3] simply claim that "the mey is the Turkish name, duduk the Armenian term, for an ancient woodwind instrument that also includes the balaban of Central Asia and the Chinese *guan* among its varieties," i.e., that they are simply different names for the same instrument. Although all these instruments share obvious similarities in construction, such an approach greatly undermines the most significant elements, which form the individuality of an instrument. It takes no account of meanings that have been developed over years for each instrument, because of limited contact with the people who construct, play, and change the instrument of the other culture. For seventy years Armenia has been a member of the Soviet Union, a battlefield of social forces unique to it. The duduk has absorbed a whole array of cultural

"knowledges," which await their release for a role in the construction
of new meanings, dependent on context and discourse.

So far, the duduk's meaning has been focused around its national
identity. All those meanings dependent on context are heavily inter-
textual and rely on discourse focused around its role in the articulation
of the concept of nation. It is in this way that cultural memory becomes selective. The stark contrast between the instrument's physical
fixity and the highly adaptable nature of the meaning production
mechanism it relies on makes it susceptible to becoming a tool for
meaning-manipulation.

According to Pavlich, a rabis player in Leninakan, "the duduk is
played everywhere where there were Armenians at some time or
other." An employee at Armenian Radio felt that "if the duduk was
not Armenian, she did not know what was." Gasparyan spoke to me
with great passion of the Armenianness of the duduk: "the duduk is
ours, a few hundred years ago, there was no Georgian duduk player.
Where Armenians went, those countries began playing."

But how does this identity of the duduk influence the view of
duduk playing? Gasparyan went on to explain that "a foreigner can
learn the duduk and play it extremely well and people will like it, but
he can never get to the essence of it, because he is not Armenian.[4] He
has not grown up in these surroundings. It is not in his blood." Using
Dikoetter's typologies of nationalism we may classify such an attitude
under "racial nationalism" whereby the significance of a "pseudo-
biological entity united by blood" acquires inordinately high rank in
the eyes of the members of the nation. In such a conception of nation,
"national culture is perceived to be the product of a racial essence"
(Dikoetter 1996, 591-92). With this as a starting point, the conforma-
tion of Armenianness to playing technique is facilitated, as the concept of Armenianness in duduk music becomes determined by the
player, not by his playing. Thus, it becomes easier to endow elements
which were previously of little symbolic value with the label "Armenian," the ambiguous nature of these elements offering the means of
manipulating them. Who could prove that the rendering of slow sad
songs heavily ornamented with melismata through the velvety sound
of the duduk is not uniquely Armenian?[5] Or that sadness as an element
of duduk playing was not uniquely Armenian? In the words of Gasparyan: "if a man has had a good life, he cannot play the duduk well,
it is just not possible."[6]

I hope I have been able to demonstrate that despite the possibilities of ambiguity inherent in the construction of similar instruments in

neighbouring countries, Armenian national identity has ensured that it retains its distinctiveness. The only way for us to objectively defend and assess this distinctiveness is by emphasizing the value of meaning over the stability of construction or the equivocality of its sonorous characteristics.

What is crucial for a reading of the following chapters is the distinction between this centrality of national identity in discourse or certain contexts and the inconsistency of its capacity to pervade meanings constructed in given contexts. The funeral, for instance, is endowed with a mood, which renders the central interpretation of duduk sounds as "sadness." I view this as a denotation, readily contrasted with connotations which are more the "possibilities" of other meanings which should not be excluded. These possibilities may range from something unusual, such as the type of affect conveyed if those present are aware of the love the deceased may have had for the duduk or music in general, to something far more common, such as the associations one of the themes played by the duduk players may activate.

It is the connotations, which, being more stable, are appropriated and adapted to notions of national identity. "The Armenians are a sad people, the duduk is a sad instrument, therefore the duduk is Armenian. The spirit of Armenia is in its people, working and living on the land, the duduk is a rural instrument, therefore the duduk is most Armenian." Such are the thoughts and discourse which freely adopt meanings derived in contexts, themselves unrelated to conceptions of nation, and use them to reinforce already present notions of identity.

Notes

1. Armenians are quick to point out differences between duduk and zurna.

2. I use as my basis for this thesis, the idealization of a specifically Armenian style of playing which is evidenced through Gasparyan's portrait of his duduk technique. The development of elements which are portrayed as uniquely Armenian depend on their separability from elements used elsewhere. It is not surprising that the concept of "an Armenian way of playing the duduk" has flourished since the duduk came into contact with the "outside world." Does this not suggest that greater contact will require and impel the use of newer and more refined elements that can be used as demarcators?

3. At the time I found this page on the internet, there was no date, and the full title was "Basic Info for Mey or Duduk," by David Brown.

3. At the time I found this page on the internet, there was no date, and the full title was "Basic Info for Mey or Duduk," by David Brown.

4. Compare with Bruno Nettl in his "29 Issues and Concepts": "You will never understand this music. There are things that every Persian on the street understands instinctively which you will never understand, no matter how hard you try" (1983, 259).

5. Frank Dikoetter's typologies are essentially useful, but can also be greatly misleading. Dikoetter seems to imply that cultural nationalism and racial nationalism are mutually exclusive, and essentially contrasting phenomena:

> Cultural nationalists seek to integrate and harmonize notions of tradition and modernity in an evolutionary vision of the community. In contrast, the positing of an immutable biological essence, based on a patrilineal line of descent, allows racial nationalists to explicitly reject tradition and culture and embrace a vision of modernity in an iconoclastic attack on the past while preserving a sense of national uniqueness. (Dikötter 1996, 591-92)

Dikoetter is concerned here with extreme cases. In the case of Armenia, as presented through the words of Gasparyan, the two typologies are not so clearly separable. Gasparyan's belief that "if it is not in the blood, one cannot understand the duduk" in no way implies a rejection of tradition and culture. It merely provides a means of re-inventing this tradition and culture in a new sociopolitical environment.

6. It will be shown later that this melancholy that is associated with the suppressed nation is also associated very closely with the duduk. This makes sadness as a quality associated almost exclusively with the duduk (among wind instruments) very important in establishing the Armenianness of the duduk. This relation between sadness, national identity, and music is far from unique to Armenia. Speaking of Hungary, Gunther Eyck notes:

> It may seem. . . odd that a poem of elegy and passivity should become the anthem of a strongly nationalist and ethnocentric people, known for their vivacity and dash. . . Quite possibly, the ever present melancholia has been conditioned by the cultural and geopolitical isolation which like a plasm had enveloped Hungarians for centuries.

Also an interview that appeared in the New York Times on June 24, 1991, quoted Hungarian Premier Joszef Antall as saying: "A Hungarian will always see the worst. . . Every renewal in our history was always born in pessimism. . . . Even our anthem is pessimistic" (Eyck 1995, 101-14).

Part 3

Context as Prime Determinant of Meaning

Having noted the role of context in the creation of meaning, let us examine specific cases more closely. I have divided contexts into domains of solo playing (including small ensembles like duduk-drone-dhol) and ensemble playing—the case of the folk orchestra. Such a division employs as its criterion playing technique rather than meaning per se, as understood so far. I find this useful firstly because any attempts at categorizing meanings will inevitably give rise to complications, primarily due to the inconsistency of its function, and secondly because playing technique (which is after all, an important tool in the creation of meaning) is increasingly diverging in two distinct directions determined by our two categories.

Chapter 7

Solo Duduk Playing

Rabis: Funerals

The term *rabis* is difficult to define on account of the varied situations in which it is used. It is short for *Rabboche Izkouztva* [Russian: literally worker's art]. Whoever attempts a definition of rabis usually begins by saying, "it is the low quality stuff. You know, musicians of the lowest standard." Vahan compared it with the Greek *skiladiko*, also considered by most to be "a low form of music." Alexander Djumaev (from whom I adopted the spelling) describes it as "The Professional Union of Art Workers" (1993, 43). This definition was in fact the official Soviet one. In current usage however, it is more common to employ the word to designate the folk music played in a pop setting with pop instrumentation in Armenia. This same term is used in a different way to describe the duduk players (and their location) who are hired for funerals (probably because the players were members of the professional union in Soviet times).

Despite the derogatory use of the word, the music played by duduks at funerals is loved and respected. To present an idea of the capacity of funerals for the creation of affect, meaning, and mood, I will attempt to portray, in the form of a narrative, the situation a particular funeral gave rise to.

Funerals in Armenia are usually separable into two episodes: a wake at the house of the deceased, indoors, and the burial at the cemetery. The same two duduk players (the number depends on the financial ability of the hirer but is usually two) play in both these settings, and their roles are well-defined. The melody player will always play, but not necessarily decide the melody to play, and the drone player will always accompany. Much of the music is played standing up or while walking, and even outdoors, the sound is kept fairly soft.

I recall in great lucidity my first attendance of a funeral. I was accompanied by a friend, Barkev Parsekhian, who happily disclosed all information pertaining to the occasion. He explained that we were going to the "taghoumi bureau" (burials office) where people would come to report a death, and then if they wished to, make all the necessary arrangements of the funeral, including the hiring of duduk players. "There is a special room," he said, "where until eleven o'clock in the morning duduk players sit and wait for someone to give them a deposit, time, and location."

We arrived at the central taghoumi bureau in Yerevan, which is apparently and understandably considerably larger than the others. It was an old building in desperate need of renovation, as is the case with most buildings in Yerevan, blessed with the sounds of a noisy central street and the smell of dust in its corridors. Across the bureau, in the park, there was a designated area where people, some holding their duduks, others not, were walking about in search of customers. We walked through them, and were repeatedly stopped and asked what we needed. It felt much like a taxi stand where taxis are waiting for the passenger to come along. I asked my friend why there were so many of them. Were there so many burials every day? How high would the birth rate have to be if the central office of a town of 1,500,000 had so many deaths? The hiring of a large number of duduk players or ensembles for a single funeral was not only a means of expressing respect for the deceased (if the financial means were available), but also an assertion of social standing. At the lower end of the financial ladder, two players were the tacitly accepted norm. A single duduk player is a relative rarity, since as is realized by player and customer alike, "it is better not to have anyone at all, than to have a duduk without a *dam* [drone]" (Pavlich).

Arriving at the bureau, we found two duduk players awaiting the particulars (time and place) of an impending assignment. Raising no objection to my presence at the funeral, they advised me to sit on a bench until they knew more. We drove to the house of the deceased's family, where at the entrance we noted a small crowd of people sitting silently and lost in thought, with the only sounds present being those of children playing in the park opposite the house. Hovhannes opened the glove compartment and retrieved the two duduks, as well as the case for the reeds. Upon seeing us, faces acquired interrogatory expressions, which were relaxed once our identity as the duduk players was confirmed. Their moment of excitement had passed away. We were only the duduk players.

Soon the request arrived that we should proceed upstairs, so we entered an apartment crowded with people. There was immense commotion as though all those present had endless errands to attend to. The stairs outside the house were also in heavy traffic, but the agitation was dominated by the sound of women wailing and periodically shouting words of mild reproach to the deceased for being the source of their suffering. The large number of people and the smallness of the house made the level of noise almost unbearable. Hovhannes asked for a separate room if possible, stating that this was the custom. The host seemed aware of this fact, and had left the bedroom door locked. We went in and Hovhannes asked for seats.

The playing began with the well known and, as it seems, almost inevitable *Hovern Yelan*. This song is often heard on the duduk, perhaps because of Gasparyan's rendering in *The Last Temptation of Christ*, a highly controversial film which caused a stir in many religious communities, thereby receiving more attention than expected (Connelly 1993, 125). *Hovern Yelan*, whether it deserves its current status in the repertoire or not, is doubtless the most performed piece on the duduk in Armenia today. The need for pieces and their performance to express that sadness, which is inherent in such occasions, was fulfilled with remarkable effortlessness. Indeed little of the duduk repertoire fails to conform to this need. A great number of the songs concern longing or loss in love or exile from the Armenian homeland.

The music proceeded with small or no pauses until the crowd began descending the stairs, followed by the coffin. We followed behind, playing while walking, until the coffin was placed in the car, and preparations were made for the drive to the cemetery.

At the entrance to the cemetery, we joined the procession, walking immediately behind the coffin. The music did not stop until the digging began. The digging was watched in silence, except for the loud chirping sounds of the cicadas, distant barking of dogs, and barely audible sounds of suppressed weeping. The intensely red soil, colored by a powerful sun, gave the day a summery feel, which, under the circumstances, seemed more oppressive than refreshing. As the coffin was lifted, in order to be lowered into the earth, the duduks were sounded once again. People would sometimes look at the coffin, and sometimes at the duduk players. Not long after, the music ceased giving way to speeches and drinks in honor of the deceased.

On our way back, I asked Hovhannes, the melody player, in which countries the duduk was played. He was not sure, but he was able to tell me that it "is not played only in Armenia—although it is of course Armenian, but in Georgia and Azerbaijan, and other countries too." "Which other countries?" I enquired. "All countries which have been suppressed by foreign powers [*jnshvatz yergirner*]" he answered, with a deep sigh.

According to Hovhannes, the playing of duduks at funerals was not popular during Soviet times. It is generally agreed however, that it is a very old Armenian custom. The general movement towards what is perceived to be pre-Soviet patterns discernible on the duduk (discussed in part 2) has helped re-introduce it at funerals. The funeral is not only a vehicle for the use of elements unique to solo playing (such as melismata, vibrati, and slides), but is also a medium for the communication and construction of the "sadness characteristic" whose subsequent verbal association with the Armenian nation strengthens the duduk's iconic value, while adding to its capacity as demarcator. Just as mood is created by musical sadness, musical sadness is created by mood.

Sadness

"In its tiny holes [the duduk] bears the cry of Armenia's bitter past" (Djivan Gasparyan).[1] "[The duduk] is not a happy instrument, it is most certainly not a happy instrument" (Barkev Parsekhian). "How well this instrument expresses the sadness of our land" (Hovhannes). "The only music the duduk can really play well, is sad music" (Pavlich). "The duduk is a sad instrument" (Vahan Kalstian).

Khachaturian is often quoted as having said that "the duduk is the only instrument that can make me cry." Although it is often said that the duduk is at once the happiness and the sadness of Armenia, the happiness actually refers to the pride it gives the Armenian, whereas the sadness is a description of the type of music which has come to be most closely associated with it, as well as the instrument's distinctive sound in the rendering of such pieces. The repertoire of the solo duduk, is today comprised mostly of songs, a good number of which, are sad songs. It is true that *moughamats*[2] (maqams) are sometimes played on the duduk and the dance repertoire is far from unknown to it. However, funerals are much more the perceived home of the duduk than are weddings, or other "happy" events such as baptisms, anniversaries, etc. The zurna and clarinet are always preferred in such occasions because of the less "melancholy" sounds produced by them, and especially because of their loudness.[3] The duduk is preferred for occasions when a softer sound is necessary. With increasing availability of microphones and loudspeakers, the volume of sound may not be a problem in the future, but at present expenses are kept to a minimum in Armenia, and these are avoided.[4]

On one occasion, Vahan told me that "the zurna can be played by anyone, it is a happy instrument and everybody knows how to have a good time, but not everyone can play the duduk. The duduk demands more of the player. It is a serious instrument." It may be worth enquiring here why sad music is taken more "seriously" than dance music, or happy music. Indeed, an enquiry into the nature of "sad music" might shed some light on our understanding of not only the function of the duduk in the context of funerals, but also of the way in which meaning is constructed and manipulated through discourse and instruments' peculiar susceptibility to meaning changes. The duduk's unmistakable and consistent association with sad music or the tendency throughout Armenia of referring to it as a "sad instrument" raise some questions about how such notions are developed and foregrounded in society.

First, let us question what sad music is. Or rather, why certain music is described as sad. The recent literature seems to suggest that sad music is not referred to as sad because it makes the listener sad. Jerrold Levinson speaks of an imaginary concertgoer whose experience "can be described—at least provisionally—as intense grief, unrequited passion, sobbing melancholy, tragic resolve, and angry despair." He then asks "why would anyone in effect torture himself in this manner?" (Levinson 1990, 306). Making an exception, then for masochists, if this were the case, no one would listen to sad music. Certainly there are people who would avoid music which is sad, simply because they cannot bear it, because it makes them sad, but such people are more the exception than the rule.[5] It is also agreed that sad music is not always evocative of some particular sad incident (although sometimes it is). Levinson argues that if what we call a "sadness-reaction" was characterized by some "memory image of a particular earlier sadness," then the particulars of that occasion (such as time, place, etc.) would come to mind when listening. But we are not. A listener's capacity for feeling sadness from music may be "exercised and deepened" by sadness-experiences in life, but this does not imply that listeners "could not possibly be saddened by music if they had not been saddened outside of music," in other words, a sadness-reaction is not necessarily, if at all, a recollection of a sad incident in the listener's life. John Hospers portrays sadness as a depersonalized element of music, i.e., one which is "taken out of or abstracted from, the particular personal situation in which we ordinarily feel it," citing the "death of a loved one" and the "shattering of one's hopes" as examples of the context in which "sadness in life" is felt. The element of sadness in music, on the other hand, is for Hospers what is sometimes called the "essence" of sadness "without all the accompanying accidents or causal conditions which usually bring it into being." In other words, music expresses sadness, but "we should distinguish the music-sadness, which is a happy experience, from life sadness which is not"(Hospers 1969, 152), an argument which essentially retains the form given to it by Aristotle's discourse on tragedy.

Both these theses depend partly on the idea that music is removed from "real-life sadness," as is usually the case in Western classical music, whereas the duduk is played at funerals where this real-life sadness is not only alive but very much the predominant mood. However, we should not dismiss these arguments on such grounds since they are statements about sad music in general, not only Western sad music, and although they use the case of classical music as their basis, I suggest that the points they make are not limited to Western music. Nor are these arguments irrelevant since they help us to understand that it is not only the present-day association of the duduk with funerals that is responsible for the duduk as being perceived as a sad instrument. It would be equally acceptable to say that the duduk is played in funerals because it is a sad instrument.[6] Indeed, its presence at funerals is best explained by the attitude that an occasion requires an appropriate music.

So it is not a particular image of sadness that is evoked. But a general mood of sadness, or possibly "musical analogues of [sadness]."[7] And this is why we call the music sad—not because of any sadness that it conjures up, but because of a mood of sadness to be differentiated from sadness that arises from it. So why does sad music move us so deeply? Levinson gives a convincing explanation by claiming that one of the rewards one gets from listening to sad music is related to a person's "self-respect or sense of dignity as a human being." His argument depends on the thesis that "the capacity to feel deeply" is central to most people's image of themselves. It is music's power to place us in the "feeling state of a negative emotion without its unwanted life consequences," that allows us to safely reassure ourselves "of the depth and breadth of our ability to feel" (Levinson

1990, 306-335). Vahan's views, as expressed by his phrase "everybody knows how to have a good time," are echoed in Levinson's: "It is usually not emotions like joy, amusement, or excitement that we have a need of proving ourselves equal to and prepared for feeling." Levinson has rested his argument on a shared notion of what constitutes "an emotionally developed individual."

Levinson's argument shows the centrality of respect in sad music. Of course he speaks only of self-respect, but his conclusion can easily be extended to include respect towards the duduk and those who play it. Our ability "to feel deeply" is provided by the duduk, therefore it is respected more than an instrument (or music) which provides us with those "emotions like joy, amusement, or excitement." It is this respect, which is employed in separating the duduk from other instruments that are known throughout the East (*arevelian kortzikner*).[8] The duduk is thus assigned a high status among folk instruments.

A very important role in conveying the element of sadness through the duduk is played by its highly valued timbre. Gasparyan speaks of the greatness of this timbre, and how it did not exist before he became famous. "Before me do you know how people played the duduk? Like this:" He blows the duduk and makes a brassy or saxophone-like sound, similar to that of the zurna. "But now they play like this": this time the characteristic velvety sound comes out.[9] "They may as well have played like this," he jokes, using the duduk as a drumstick and beating time with it. As is evident from the earlier recordings of the solo duduk, Gasparyan was exaggerating. The sound of the duduk throughout the earlier recordings is more nasal than it is today (closely resembling that of the mey in the 1970s), but never strident as Gasparyan portrayed it.

Clearly, Khachaturian would not have shed tears if the duduk were not a sad instrument. But it is, as we have seen from the above arguments, not actually sadness which made him cry. Peter Kivy identifies the beauty of the music as the quality which "elicits the tears," not the sorrow: "These are not tears of sadness, sorrow or melancholy."[10] Indeed they are not. But they come from a beauty which is made all the more profound (following Levinson's argument) due to the presence of a mood of sadness. The absence of a mood of sadness would have left the beauty bereft of some of this profoundness and solemnity, and thereby changed the nature of the beauty.

Regardless of the reasons why sadness in music is so attractive, Gasparyan's words portray the significance of discourse in the creation of meaning: "We've had happy moments, but the majority of our existence has been a life of oppression. That has definitely influenced our music. I too wonder, "why is our music so sad?" But that's how we are . . . Armenian people are born into sadness."[11] That Armenians view themselves as an unfortunate people is no great surprise in view of their history. "The refrain of one well known Armenian song, addressed by an Armenian far from home to a crane flying overhead, [asks] 'Do you bring good news from our land?' But this is expressed with such doleful melancholy that it is clear the singer already knows the answer to the question" (Walker 1980, 11).

What has happened here? Does the word "sad" express the music? Is it an analogy to other forms of sadness? Or is it a generalization prompted by the necessity of limited vocabulary and language? Why use the same word to describe the death of a loved one and the mood created by the sounds of the duduk? And is there truly a relation between the duduk's Armenianness and its sadness simply because the loop is nicely completed by claiming that Armenians are a sad people?

Meaning and context are not only inseparable, but they continually reconstruct each other. Cultural knowledge becomes cultural memory when it has to adapt to new contexts. Thus the duduk's meaning is constructed through its presence at funerals, whence it derives its sadness characteristic as an intrinsic attribute without which the duduk cannot even be thought of. The fact that this is the very instrument which in the past (before it acquired its sophisticated sound) was played with drone and dhol much like the zurna, demonstrates the effects of the selectivity of cultural memory.

The Recording Studio and Hoki

The relatively alien but highly influential context of the recording studio has appeared in recent years for the solo duduk. At once an arena of technique display and personal capacity, it provides a medium for new aesthetic discoveries, which in the absence of the heightened technical and musical standard afforded by recording would scarcely have acquired such prominence. Possibly through imitation of Western models, but also on account of new foundations that give the idea of perfection a centrality and make it the norm, an aesthetic realm has arisen in which expression in an intense form is cultivated for its own sake.

Gasparyan's successes and cheaper/improved recording technology have rendered the production and sale of duduk music a financially viable endeavour. The markets aimed for—notably the Western world music sector and the Armenian diaspora in the West, have created certain expectations which must be fulfilled. The Western perspectives on authenticity and expression have thus been foregrounded in the hope that they conform to the attitudes of buyers.

Among the vocabulary that such an adoption of values has given rise to, an important place is occupied by *hoki*. Although translating hoki is no enviable task, the *Comprehensive Dictionary Armenian-English* has come up with "soul, spirit, ghost, person; the Holy Ghost; life, fiend, goblin; individual." In addition, *hoki dal* (literally "to give hoki") means "to animate," *hokin pchel* (literally "to blow the hoki")—to expire, or die away (Kouyoumdjian 1970, 431).

The applicability of this word in a number of differing situations means that to speak of it simply as "soul" would not be adequate. The concept of hoki can be used universally in the music of Armenia, but its use when speaking of wind instruments is especially important. The fact that one may speak of "blowing" the hoki, gives the word a special significance to wind players. The idea of putting one's soul in the music (which is as common in Armenia as it is in English-speaking countries) becomes more palpable for wind players, who can almost literally achieve it. One feels this palpability most in the melismata. Among wind instruments, one may safely say that the concept is most closely associated with the duduk.

The idea of hoki rests on its indefiniteness. Hoki cannot be defined, and therefore successfully eludes the hegemony of discourse. But this is a rise to the ethereal, a complete resignation to the standards and values offered by a purely aesthetic orientation to folk music. According to Vahan, it is "one of those difficulties which cannot be overcome by just anyone." It requires "that something from within." Djivan Gasparyan spoke of endless hours of practice, for those who actually had "something inside." He insisted however that "those people who [had] nothing inside, may spend all day on the instrument, they will achieve nothing—hoki does not come with practice."

Exactly where hoki is most valued, is not a matter of general agreement. Some believe that it is necessary for phrasing well. Others associate it with the sound quality. A rabis duduk player, Hovannes Hagopian, spoke with much fervour on the subject, expressing his belief that it was impossible to create any sound out of the duduk without hoki. "Of course," he said, "it is not entirely impossible, for example it is very easy to create an ugly sound, or an unbecoming sound, if one has no hoki, but one cannot play the duduk with such sounds. It needs something from inside."

It seemed to me however, that for most players, hoki was principally considered necessary for the execution of the melismata[12] (in Armenian, *melism*; plural, *melismner*). The *Harvard Dictionary* defines melisma as "an expressive vocal passage sung to one syllable, as opposed to a virtuoso-like and frequently stereotyped coloratura." The *Oxford Dictionary* defines it as a "term used to describe a group of notes sung to one syllable of the text." Finally Grove's defines it as a "group of more than five or six notes sung to a single syllable." Although one often speaks of melismatic passages, the use of the term for a passage played on an instrument rather than sung, is not mentioned by any of the above. The word "melism" is used by the musicians to denote a passage where the notes don't fully sound and resemble a trill which includes more than two pitches. Since the duduk is, in most cases, imitating a song, or at any rate rendering a song, we may conclude that its use for an instrumental passage is appropriate. In any case, this word, which was introduced to Armenia from the West via Russia, is widely used by the players themselves, who understand it more or less in the same way as people understand it in the West.[13]

Few pieces if any are played on the duduk without melismata. In very fast dances, the line between melisma and fast passage becomes very blurred, for which reason its value in this context is somewhat limited.[14] But the significance of the melismata are greatest in the slower, sad songs, since it is here that they are most conspicuous, and provide an excellent contrast to the rest of the piece. These contrasts are in some ways perfectly suited to the mood, since they don't divert one's attention from the overall elegiac nature of the piece. They provide a reinforcement of the hoki. Hagopian feels that the more the melismata, the greater the hoki of the player, if executed well, and when appropriate.

Vahan demonstrated his method of producing effective melismata to me, and claimed that this technique was to be used as a basis, and its refinement could only be achieved if one used his hoki. This endows hoki with a certain individuality (another Western attribute?). From my observations, it seemed that Vahan was using his epiglottis to alternately block and unblock his windpipe very quickly, so that this process could be repeated three or four times a second. He claimed that it was a secret and that "no duduk player will ever tell you how to achieve a melisma since it will have taken him too many years of work for that." He also added that "to produce a good melisma, it is important to blow from 'deep inside' otherwise the sound will be too shallow." It is perhaps somewhat unusual that the fingers are given hardly any credit for the execution of these passages. They are mere accessories. This is partly explained by the fact that the concept of hoki is closely associated in duduk playing with blowing, since both can be thought of as coming from inside. If the execution of a melisma is an expression of hoki, as Vahan implies, then it seems likely that blowing will be especially valued at the expense of fingering.

As recalcitrant to language as hoki and melisma may seem, they are ultimately a construction through discourse, which owes a lot to Western hegemony. They are a final departure from functionality and owe their raison d'être to the polish of the new context: the studio.

Duduk Competitions

The rise of an annual duduk competition furnishes duduk playing with its most recent context. Compared with most competitions around the world, music related or otherwise, it is highly primitive, betraying a lack of experience on the parts of organizers, judges, and participants. It was begun in 1998 on the initiative of National Radio (possibly at the suggestion of Gasparyan) with the intention of promoting talented young duduk players and the duduk itself, although many players claim that its principle goal was to provide the radio with fine players recording duduk music for free.

Chairman of the jury in both 1998 and 1999 was Gasparyan, who exercised barely challenged control over the decisions, although debates among the jury members were highly common. There were no established criteria to assist with decision making, no set pieces, and no regulations to limit the number of participants. Players were sometimes dismissed by Gasparyan on the sounding of a single note on the grounds that a performer who begins in such a manner is no performer at all. "Try again next year," was his palliative solution. As uncertainty of the general standard remained, decisions continued to be inconsistent.

Participants often arrived from remote parts of Armenia, which in light of their financial difficulties demonstrates their faith in the competition for offering prestige and career development. Ages varied from ten or eleven year olds to eighteen or nineteen. At the start of their performance, they were asked to present themselves by declaring name, town or village, age and master's name. Often, rural regions provided a subject for tacit derision on the part of some jury members.

If the players were recognized, or known, Gasparyan could declare that they need not play, as he had heard them before. Objections were not raised in the case of his approval of such players (the prize winners of the previous competition for instance), but when the grounds for not listening were that they were not good performers, arguments in the presence of the candidate made for highly unusual scenes. The unfortunate candidate awaiting the decision was forced to hear conversations of a quasi-philosophical nature where the criteria decided could favor him or reject him.

Debates were even more common on the subject of the rendering of certain pieces. Participants were not informed in advance of any particular pieces, or even genres of pieces. On entering they were heard playing a piece of their own choice, usually one of the well known lyrical pieces. They were then asked to provide a contrasting piece, usually a fast dance. Some candidates claimed not to have prepared a fast dance, in which case they were either rejected on the grounds that duduk players should have all-round repertoires, or asked to play a slow dance, which would not show off their technical abilities, a fact that was usually interpreted as not *having* technical abilities.

In the case of well-known pieces, improvisation was a common subject for debate. If players improvised excessively, it was uncertain whether this was because they intentionally engaged in highly imaginative interpretations of the piece, or whether they simply lost their way, and could not play it. Jury members' inconsistency in distinguishing between the two moulded the creation of criteria and norms, which by the end of the competition were established to such a degree that they were considered natural and perennial. All pieces had to be rendered with no decorating or improvising once, and could then be repeated freely to demonstrate the players spontaneity and imagination.

In all, the 1999 competition was much akin to rituals where the negotiation of identity marks all actions taken, whether on behalf of Gasparyan, his subordinate jury members or players. A struggle to demonstrate knowledge, ability, and an attempt to improve or maintain status characterized decision-makings in the same way that it featured in performances.

What meaning does the duduk acquire in such contexts? It itself becomes the context of negotiations, a site where quality and ability are determined. Player and instrument here are barely separable for the release of meaning. The duduk, in the presence of competitors, becomes an embodiment of the competitive spirit. It is not long before it is seen as an instrument capable of presenting a performer's greatest achievements and is therefore accorded high status itself. Its association with finesse and quality (despite the rather untidy staging of the competition) make it a "worthy" instrument. Language does the rest. The instrument becomes worthy of a national status. If national culture is used as a means of competing with other national cultures, its representative forms must be worthy contestants.

Special Events

In a number of national celebrations staged for various purposes (national holidays, independence day, etc.), concerts take place where traditional music and dance constitute a significant share of the event. These events may last several hours and either take place in the afternoon or evening. They are mostly held in concert halls, although in the summer, outdoor venues too are common.

It is very common to have both musicians and dancers appear in traditional dress, comprised of highly elaborate and colorful designs. Such regalia are seminal in the construction of rural places, a central aim of producers. Duduk players usually appear in the perceived "standard" traditional context of the duduks and dhol ensemble, usually portrayed as shepherds. The tunes performed vary in lyricism and rhythmic intensity and are usually backgrounded by the dancing.

Audiences vary. I recall attending one such event with a friend who was a classical musician, who did not regard the quality of this music very highly, but prided himself on its Armenianness. His presence there was unrelated to aesthetic considerations and seems to have relied partly on a national identity. In an almost perverse way, one could conjecture that a belief in "aesthetic communities" (as opposed to aesthetics per se) motivated his appearance in such events.

The visual and acoustical depictions found in such events are invariably associated in urban areas with rurality. Again, meaning is derived from context which itself is constructed by specific features such as the duduk. This peculiar hermeneutic-style circle gives rise to discourse about Armenianness and rurality. As in other contexts, cultural memory is preserved through selection.

In this section, I have aimed at giving a brief overview of the essential elements and meanings of solo duduk playing. The following section on the playing of the duduk in folk ensembles will provide a view of the different concerns facing duduk players in a context, which bears little relations to those described above. This contrast I hope will portray to the reader the dichotomy between Soviet-style advancement and a return to Armenian traditions, the latter clearly but not unequivocally gaining the upper hand since the collapse of the Soviet Union. This binary opposition, however, loses its validity as soon as we shift emphasis from considerations of instrument technique (peculiar to musicians and musicologists) to considerations of meaning (common to a much larger social group). Folk ensembles are still highly regarded by most duduk players as a medium for the expression of national sentiment, a fact that supports the hypothesis that the political impositions of Soviet rule received wide-ranging acceptance in the peripheral republics on account of their representational capacity as forms of national culture.

Notes

1. As quoted in Schnabel's Rhythm Planet (Schnabel 1998, 54).

2. Maqams (see appendix C).

3. Zurnas have been known at funerals, but are rare. Poché mentions this particular function as "still surviving in Armenia and Sri Lanka" (Poché 1984, 3-907).

4. GNP per capita in Armenia is currently roughly estimated to be around four hundred dollars according to Reuters news source in a recent article related to Armenia.

5. This point, too, is generally agreed upon (see for instance Ridley 1995, 146-70).

6. This argument should not be seen as a contradiction of my previous claim that the element of "sadness" is actively sought as a means of promulgating the duduk's association with Armenia. Comparing it to the zurna, there is no doubt (throughout the earlier recordings) that the duduk sound is softer, more contemplative and intimate, disposing it to a greater degree to sadness.

7. "Those who are skeptical of the claim that music often induces familiar emotions in listeners sometimes maintain that what is induced is . . . musical analogues of the familiar emotions of life" (Levinson 1990, 315).

8. Literally: Eastern instruments, Eastern implying universal.

9.Gasparyan's words "before me" should be interpreted to mean some fifty years ago. He never suggested that Hovsepian's sound was brassy.

10. As quoted by James Hudson in an article dated November 1998 on the internet. Also: "Music can move us—by its beauty, perfection, craftsmanship, or even the excellence of its expressiveness" (Kivy 1987, 157-59)

11. Djivan Gasparyan as quoted by Schnabel (1998, 44).

12. Earlier music dictionaries tend to synonymize the word "melisma" with coloratura or fioritura for the particular case of passages in plainsong when one syllable flowers out into a passage of several notes. More recent publications actually stress the distinction: Coloratura is used more for a display of virtuosity, the melisma for expression.

13. The conservatories are the probable sources of such words used among folk musicians, and these provide Western-style training and a large number of words such as "melism" and "temperament" are to be found in their Russian forms, which are often very similar to the English or German versions. As was mentioned earlier, such terms are in all likelihood a recent adoption for the majority of duduk players (see part 2, 4).

14. This limitation may be attributed to the fact that as an expression of hoki, *melismner* are highly expressive passages which cannot really be conveyed through dance music. Even in slow music, their emotive power may easily be missed by the Westerner's "untrained" ear, since the length of the melism may on first hearing seem insufficient. Given time, however, its expressiveness becomes clear to the listener.

Chapter 8

The Folk Ensemble

The folk ensemble is normally referred to as the folk orchestra, or the folk-instruments orchestra (Rice 1994, GSE 1975, Djumaev 1993, Levin 1993). The players themselves however, reserve the term "orchestra" exclusively for the Western classical orchestra. In case of doubt, the name of the folk orchestra would suffice to clarify the type of ensemble in question.

Although today folk ensembles are common throughout the Soviet Union, the earliest recorded example dates to the 1870s. Among these earliest specimens, we find an ensemble of Vladimir horn players and the Great Russian Orchestra (which includes a large variety of folk instruments) of the end of the nineteenth century (GSE 1975, 18-513). It was only after the onset of Soviet rule, however, that these orchestras became widespread, gradually serving as a means of "advancement." Reconstructions of instruments served as a means of "developing" the orchestras (especially in the autonomous republics) and implementing the policies of Europeanization. According to the GSE, reconstructions helped "enrich the ensembles' expressive and technical means" (1975, 18-513).

The folk ensembles found all over Armenia consist of (mostly) folk instruments (with the common exceptions of cello and clarinet), conducted by the *dirijer*, a conductor who has usually also arranged or composed the music which is played, and a singer (although some pieces are purely instrumental). Most ensembles will include a number of duduks, one or two *shvins* (end-blown duct flutes made of reed or wood with seven fingerholes and a thumbhole), a clarinet, a cello, a *davough* (10-stringed harp), a *kanun* (72-stringed zither), a dhol (frame-drum), and two *kemantchas* (spike fiddles similar to the *rabab* of Egypt, or *Joze* of Iraq). Both Arsen's and Vahan's ensembles included four duduks, the only instrument to have more than one or two representatives. This is probably partly due to its soft sound, but may also be attributed to its great popularity at present. In all the examples I encountered, the conductor was classically trained and likely to be conducting the symphony orchestra the week after conducting the folk ensemble.

The importance of the ensemble to duduk players cannot be overemphasized as all duduk players, with very few exceptions, play in one. Margaryan, who is, as we have noted, widely regarded as "the first great duduk player," played in one of the earlier ensembles, and went to the extent of learning notation to conform to the changing requirements. Similarly (in later generations), Gasparyan played in the Taloul Altounian ensemble for eighteen years.

Another reason for the centrality of the ensemble in the life of duduk players is the instrument's general absence in Western-style solo recitals, common in the performance of classical music. Regardless of its stature and its image as a highly expressive instrument, the concept of a full-length solo recital devoted to a folk instrument has not yet emerged from the complex array of continual restructuring which has repeatedly redefined the changing status of the idea of a folk instrument. Today, the duduk is regarded as a concert instrument mainly within the context of the folk ensemble (its somewhat different positions in the recording studio and special events notwithstanding), in contrast to its status as a rabis instrument at funerals, but its increasing prominence in the recording studio might help the establishment of new venues supporting the development of the solo image of this instrument. Until such time, however, the folk ensemble offers the duduk an attractive haven where it can retain its professionalism and concert status.

I spent many days with Arsen, attending rehearsals of the folk ensemble of which he is a proud member. "The Aram Merangulian ensemble," he says "is not only the first ensemble ever to have come into existence (in 1926), but also by far the best professional ensemble around."[1] The Soviet use of the word "professional" complied well with the common notion of "that by which one makes one's living," but its penetration into the nineties whose economic climate has not permitted a retainment of the established Soviet norms for the salariat, raises the question of why folk ensembles still exist. Arsen claims that he earns ten dollars per month playing in the ensemble, a sum, which compared with the twenty dollars a day he earns playing the clarinet at the restaurant is almost negligible. Nevertheless, he and his fellow players attend every rehearsal (or at least they did while I was there), and it seems, enjoy their time there.

It must be understood that the ensemble has so long been the way of life for musicians that rehearsals are very much a social event rather than a professional one. According to Arsen, "the folk orchestra was never a way of making money, it was just something you did." In addition it offers the musicians trips to Europe and America, as well as Asia, free hotels, etc., which would otherwise be unattainable.

The ensemble carries for most players prestigious connotations. Belonging to one is a mark of distinction. Wherever I met duduk players, even in the poverty-stricken city of Leninakan (whose present fate was decided in the 1988 earthquake that devastated the whole of the region, and from which Leninakan has far from recovered), the first statement about their lives was the ensemble they played in. Even Gasparyan, of his own accord, stated his ensemble career in the earlier stages of our interview.

National status has thus endowed a way of life or profession with distinction and moral soundness. It not only provides players with a medium for expression and construction of identity, but also allows for an interaction with the transcendental idea of nation, the provision of cultural substance to a large community.

The Aram Merangulian ensemble rehearses in a building whose entrance resembles a parking lot, though I could happily argue that it has no entrance at all. The players gather there every weekday, and sometimes weekends, at eleven in the morning, waiting for the arrival of their dirijer. The rehearsal may last until one o'clock in the afternoon, maybe more. In the waiting period, I would often begin conversing with one or other of the players. Arsen's three fellow *duduka-hars* were naturally the most attentive to my questions. Their leader would in moments of silence approvingly nod his head to convey his support of my bizarre but worthy project of learning more about the duduk. "*Maladiets*" (Russian for bravo), he would exclaim in his excitement, "you have come to the right place. We are the best ensemble in Armenia."[2] The shvin player had a seemingly unusual background. He related how he played the clarinet in the opera for fifteen years before joining the ensemble. "It is better to play in the ensemble," he said, "it has a better atmosphere." As the pay was not a determinant factor in the choice of orchestras, players preferred the more relaxed environment of the ensemble to the more strenuous but "finer" classical orchestra.[3] (I should note that despite the Soviets, the word "classi-cal" (klassik) has always been used by musicians and listeners alike, to denote what we understand by Western classical music). Undoubt-edly, classical music and the classical orchestra are viewed by almost everyone as more prestigious. Arsen always presented me to people with great pride, usually remembering to state that I was a pianist, but that now I wanted to be a duduk player. Nevertheless, the shvin player, although one of a minority who have come to folk music via classical, represents a gradually growing category of musicians.

During my stay, two conductors were in charge of the orchestra. The first, Rupen Sarkissian, a man in his fifties, usually serious, but always ready for a joke, was "by profession" (as he asserted), a com-poser. His instrument was the violin, and he had a prodigious selection of string pieces in his oeuvre. He thought of himself as essentially a classical composer, whose most recent compositions were twelve-tone (Schoenbergian twelve-tone style, as he pointed out), which, at least on paper looked genuinely fascinating. But, being so absorbed in clas-sical music, I wondered how he came to write for folk instruments. "Oh!" he said, "I know these instruments so well, I've been writing for so many years now for this ensemble . . ." "Yes," I thought, "but do you actually play any folk instruments yourself?" "No, I don't, but you know, in so many years of conducting, I know these instruments better than the players themselves. I often tell them how to play a pas-sage or other. This happens when you compose and conduct for an ensemble for so many years." "What are you working on at the mo-ment?" I enquired. "You know, it's good that you mentioned that, I am actually working on a duduk concerto (for duduk and folk ensem-ble)."

I should point out that duduk concertos are not at all common[4] and this particular one was commissioned. Duduk concertos may prove to be a more common genre in coming years, partly depending on the course of the development of the concept of the solo duduk. Several specimens of the "mini-concerto" genre had been introduced in the Soviet era, usually in the form of a song, where the duduk would perform a singer's role. Further research in this area may help shed light on the extent of the ensemble's influence over the ideation of the solo-duduk.

During rehearsals, Rupen sustains a fine level of respect, and the players do indeed look up to him. But he is aware of the need for a laugh, which never leaves the rehearsal room. "*Alle zusammen, bitte,*" he says. The duduks look askance at him, the kamantche player mumbles something to his neighbor. The rest of the rehearsal is dedicated by the players, to a demonstration of their own knowledge of German, a matter of no great literary appeal, I should report.

The program is nothing less than hectic, and typically includes two recordings for the radio per week, and a good number of concerts every month. In the Soviet era, radio and television were united, and the ensemble would be recorded and broadcast on both, but since their divide, the ensemble has remained in the service of the radio.

The role of leader and guide for the ensemble is assumed by the well-known and highly respected singer, Rupen Matevosian. A man of incomparable charm and matchless talent, Matevosian's popularity has been instrumental in retaining the large number of engagements offered to the ensemble. Most pieces played by the ensemble are songs, mainly sung by Rupen. Always on the lookout for international opportunities, his familiarity with the international stage is best described by an endless number of countries on his curriculum vitae. In many of these, he has been accompanied by the ensemble—all over Europe, Asia and America.

The international engagements present players with an opportunity to promote their culture and traditions through the medium of the ensemble. An Armenian observer recalls being present at their first appearance in Beirut in 1956 with great pride:

> It was a *yerki bar* (song dance) ensemble. And when they came to perform in the UNESCO building, which has three floors and seats more than a 1000, people were queuing up for tickets as far as the eye could see, and they had three concerts on three consecutive days. But it wasn't just Armenians who were there. All the Arab members of parliament and important officials were there. We were truly proud of being Armenian, then.

Arsen feels that "the ensemble is a very important kind of music group in Armenia, because the songs we play are purely Armenian." He is worried about other Armenian musicians playing foreign songs, and slowly destroying Armenian culture by doing so. "The ensemble defends Armenian culture," he says. "We play only Armenian music, and we are heard over the radio and in concerts all over the world."

The Style of Folk Ensemble Music: The Need to Make Folk Music Accessible to a Wide Audience

In the creation of the folk ensemble, propagability was a major concern. The growth of the urban population had to be accompanied by an attempt to eliminate regional idiosyncratic characteristics from folk music, which could not be understood by everyone. At the same time, as class differences were slowly transformed to differences between rural and urban society, the "more refined" tastes of the new urban population were satisfied by the more refined ways of playing folk music which served the needs of a still not fully developed urban identity. In urban areas, music had to be accessible to a large audience formed of people from diverse regions and differing tastes.

The folk ensemble not only served the needs of urbanization, but could now be used as a means of strengthening national identity through a creation of a well-defined concept of traditional music. With radios and televisions becoming more and more widespread, the music of the folk ensemble could reach every household, promulgating, for a hitherto unheard of number of people, the idea of a single national culture. For the folk ensemble to be a successful vehicle for the distribution of such ideas, its music would have to be propagable, or in musical terms, accessible.

Sarkissian told me that he always wonders how he can "make the music attractive to everyone" (unlike, I suppose, his Schoenbergian writings). The technique of writing for the folk ensemble has developed over many years, and a very refined style is evident among the works of the finest of these composers. The music often has the feel of a Khachaturian symphony, despite the fact that Khachaturian wrote little for folk instruments. He is, however, a grand figure in Armenia, and every composer who is even partly classically trained is to some degree acquainted with his works and influenced by them.

At the same time, certain jazz methods have been included. Often there are passages where each instrument is given a solo and an opportunity to demonstrate the player's virtuosity. Naturally only one of each instrument is given the solo, and in the case of the duduk this means one of four. These solos, though the folk counterparts of jazz solos, are in fact without the freedom found in jazz. The parts are precomposed and limited in length, and although their principal aim is an exhibition of skill and talent, they must conform to the aesthetic conditions imposed by the need for propagability of folk ensemble music.

Another important consideration for the composer is that the "arrangement" of the folk song adheres to the standardized original (which in this case is the song known through earlier arrangements). The duduk in solo performances almost always improvises to a great degree, and the recognition of the song by the audience is far from a priority. In the ensemble it is a priority, because in the words of Arsen, "people love to hear what they know." Although the question of what the original is, is not always clearly answered, the history of well-known songs can usually be traced back to a significant point in their standardization. An interesting example is the case of the Sayat Nova songs, which are very often played as solo pieces on the duduk and likewise as ensemble pieces. These songs, it is thought, first appeared in the eighteenth century and were transmitted from generation to generation orally, until they were written down by Nikolai Tigranian at the beginning of this century. What was written down then, and copied since, is now considered the original. To most players, who have first heard these songs on the radio or elsewhere, no other version but one that very closely resembles the Tigranian transcriptions is known.

The need for propagability thus shapes the compositional technique employed in arrangements. Harmonization as an element of advancement and an aesthetic means to accessibility has introduced new concerns for duduk players. The need to play in unison, for instance, or the need to accompany (not in unison) has arisen from the requirements of the folk ensemble. Accompanying a singer was previously known on the duduk, but only in unison. Playing a part in a larger harmonic whole has brought the art of duduk players closer to the art of Western classical instrumentalists, fulfilling at once the needs of urban culture and those of Soviet culture policy.

The Duduk: Solo Playing versus Playing in the Ensemble

In solo playing, the duduk is invariably accompanied by a drone. The consistency of this arrangement is accentuated by an idiolect, which develops on account of a certain "ownership" of either role. Players never change roles, although a drone player may be a melody player depending on the status of his partner. The drone player is often the student of the melody player, but there are many exceptions. Suggestions for the next piece to be played come from either player.

In contrast, within the context of the folk ensemble, the four players often interchange roles, although there is a leader who is often assigned a melodic line. The function of each duduk in the ensemble bears little resemblance to that of solo playing. Each player plays his part, and this may range from a harmonic bassline, to an accompaniment of the singer in unison. Thirds and sixths are often employed, the leader usually playing the higher note and one, two, or three players playing the lower note. Perhaps the most problematic passages are the ones in which the duduks are forced to play in unison.

An interesting solution to the problem of the duduk's small range is presented by the use of complimentary duduks. Each duduk player has access to two duduks, one in a high register, the other in a lower one. It often happens that two of the players play lower register duduks, while the other two provide the necessary extension into higher registers. Such an arrangement makes possible a range of nearly three octaves. The interplay of such factors offers conductors greater harmonic and compositional possibilities. As these can be implemented only through the use of notation, it is not difficult to understand why notation has in the past fifty years become an indispensable tool for the functioning of the ensemble.

Notation

The first important point to note about the source of differences between solo and ensemble playing is the use of notation. Although players know most of the songs they perform quite readily and would not hesitate if asked to play them as solo pieces, they are required to play someone else's arrangement of them. Despite the seven decades that have passed since the introduction of notation to the duduk world, today, in most cases players learn the instrument first and notation later (In order to enter the conservatory or a folk ensemble, players need to have a technicum diploma, but they may enter the technicum after school, at say the age of eighteen, for the sole purpose of getting a technicum diploma which is in itself valuable. Any institution of musical education, such as the technicum, will include in its syllabus the use of Western notation. It is there that most duduk players learn notation, usually after school).. Arsen picked up the duduk at the age of fifteen, but he claims he knew nothing of notation until the age of twenty-two when he entered the technicum. He played his first notes on the duduk by accident, just out of curiosity picking up his friend's duduk and trying it out, and he happened to recognize "the song that came out." He had had no musical education thus far, but had often played the dhol with duduk players, for fun. The pattern that his musical education followed was:

1. Arsen became acquainted with the music of duduk players by playing the dhol with them, while at the same time being generally exposed to folk music—all until the age of fifteen.
2. At fifteen he learned the duduk slowly, and by experiment, with no formal training—only advice from friends.
3. At twenty-two he decided to enter an ensemble, where a technicum diploma (hence the necessity of learning notation) was required.

It becomes clear from this pattern, which is by no means unique (with certain variations, almost all duduk players follow it), that notation is an almost superfluous addition to the already well-developed musicianship of the player. It does not facilitate the learning of songs, since by this stage the song repertoire of the players is already near completion (completion to be understood here as the acquiring of a satisfactory and necessary level of acquaintance with the well-known folk songs).[5] After this stage, the development of the duduk player as a musician is essentially unrelated to the learning of new songs, and is focused on improvisation and timbre. Thus, the learning of notation is useful only as a requirement of the folk ensemble. Despite this, players raise no objections to learning notation, regarding it as an essential step forward in their musical development.

Pitch

The technical fluency required for complete mastery over pitch has been a significant factor in establishing the duduk's image as a difficult instrument.[6] One of the difficulties often encountered is playing in unison. In many of the rehearsals I attended, the duduk players were repeatedly warned that they need to take greater care over intonation. A dissatisfied expression on the face of the conductor would often be followed by the comment: "You are out of tune with each other." Ensemble writing is inevitably furnished with a certain amount of doubling. Although Arsen claims that the "A-duduks"[7] are made such that the A is at 440 Hz, in practice, this is not true. Having demonstrated the execution of a certain passage on his duduk in our lessons, Arsen would then switch to my duduk to make sure that my incompetence was not a fault of the instrument. The only notable difference would be the sudden change in pitch. Among other factors, the unpredictability of the reed and the positioning of the bridle cause unwanted variations in pitch. Differences may be small, but in considering problems of intonation, they surface immediately.[8]

Timbre

We have already mentioned the individuality of the duduk timbre. Whether real or imagined, the centrality of the timbre in the duduk's iconic value cannot be doubted. In ensemble playing, timbre has had to undergo various forms of adaptation. Vahan recalls being told to play the duduk so that it produces a sound like a trombone. "Try," he recalls the conductor urging him, "I'm sure you can make your duduk sound like a trombone." "Why can't he just get a trombone instead and add it to the orchestra?" Vahan asks. I often observed similar problems at rehearsals I attended. The conductor once complained that "you four duduk players have been playing together for fifteen years now, and you still cannot get your timbres to match." But such requirements of adaptation have perhaps surprisingly not hindered the development of the idiosyncratic acoustical qualities of the instrument.

Meaning

The folk ensemble as context is itself placed in diverse larger contexts. Radio, television, concerts at home and abroad are all instrumental in the construction of meaning, but an analysis of the interactions of meanings in these contexts and the denotation/connotation relationships I have already emphasized would be a study in its own right. Suffice it to say, however, that national identity figures prominently in any understanding of meaning conveyed through the ensemble.

The case of television provides visual grounds for the creation of an image for the ensemble. The duduk contributes in this construct through its heightened status elsewhere (Gasparyan and the world music scene), as camera crews devote special attention to this "national pride." As embodiments of culture, instruments of the ensemble depend as much on their visual (constructional) fixity as they do on the standardization of ensemble music provided through television.

Standardization of culture is thus reinforced through a new visual dimension.

If television provides a powerful means of this standardization, an awareness of "other" articulated through the ensemble's many tours abroad provides the model. Identity is so central to meaning here, that the ensemble and its music as cultural forms are constructed for the sole purpose of creating a means to compete with "others." Such competition is perhaps the most potent motivator of musical (acoustical and visual) genres.

Notes

1. The Aram Merangulian ensemble is the only one mentioned in the *Great Soviet Encyclopedia* (1975), but not by name: "The symphony orchestra (1966) and an ensemble of native folk instruments (1926) are affiliated with radio and television" (GSE 1975, 2-353)

2. No matter what ensemble a duduk player is a member of, it is certain that he will be proud of it. Members of the Aram Merangulian ensemble claim that they are the "only professional ensemble in Armenia." Although this is in fact untrue, they are certainly the most recognized, being the first one.

3. It is a curious fact that the close relationship between classical and folk music, a result of Soviet culture policy as we have already seen (although the Soviets would prefer "professional" to "classical"), is echoed in neighboring Turkey through in some ways a similar culture policy: "Gökalp believed . . . that only one music could exist as the true, national music of Turkey, and this was to be achieved through a synthesis of Turkish folk music and the musical techniques of Western civilization" (Stokes 1992, 33-36).

4. The LP recording of a short piece written for duduk and folk ensemble which I have already mentioned should not really be classified as a concerto. The notion of a full-scale Western classical style concerto for the duduk is generally unfamiliar.

5. The repertoire that one may expect a duduk player to be familiar with consists of a small number of well-known pieces. These are employed in both solo playing and the folk ensemble. New pieces are sometimes written for the ensemble, but most compositions are arrangements of these well-known pieces.

6. A close parallel is found on the *dan nguyet* of Vietnam. Nguyen writes that "the restructuring of a pitch also implies correcting it. The fact that musicians need to correct pitches of the dan nguyet demonstrates the inappropriateness and insufficiency of its fretted pitches for a large part of the Vietnamese repertoire" (Nguyen 1986, 67). He then states that "the dan nguyet must be considered a more difficult instrument than others because of the task of pitch restructuring."

7. See appendix B for the different types of duduks. The A-duduk is the most common.

8. Playing in unison on double reed instruments is not uncommon. In Gagaku court music of Japan, for instance, the *hichiriki*, which in many ways closely resembles the duduk, traditionally plays in unison with two other hichiriki, which, like the dan nguyen of Vietnam, is partly for this reason considered a difficult instrument.

Chapter 9

Conclusion

In some ways, the relationship between duduk playing within the folk ensemble and the duduk as solo instrument in its various contexts mirrors the relationship between Soviet political impositions on a peripheral culture, and the resulting ideology emerging within the people as social group defined by this culture. In playing techniques, we find both the tensions and reconciliations inherent in the advancement/ recreation of the past binarism.

That advancement in the Soviet Union had the goal of leaving behind traditions and backward elements in an all-embracing assimilation seems to have created no obstacle in allowing advancement to be the very instrument of non-assimilation, demarcation, and erector of social boundaries. Strangely, the same may be said of the folk ensemble and its instrumentality in the construction of the past, which is now slowly taking a different path to the ensemble itself.

But despite the differences in the two paths, they are remarkably interdependent, and the construction of meaning is heavily reliant on this interdependence. Indeed, the duduk within and outside the ensemble makes a strong case for the interdependence of meanings in varying contexts. Though it has provided little resistance to the requirements of the folk ensemble, the duduk has used many of the possibilities offered by it, to develop aspects of its solo technique. The most notable example is the propagability of folk ensemble arrangements which have helped define traditional Armenian music, a concept which is of culminant importance for the development of the solo duduk's iconic value, or rather of its value as demarcator, which has motivated the development of its idiosyncrasies.

But what is traditional Armenian music? What are these traditions? Does the history of these traditions deserve the label of "continuity?" Is it possible to identify a logical development of traditions through the Soviet era? In 1962, Matossian wrote that "contrasts between secular and traditional ways persisted in post-war Armenia" (1962, 177), and indeed for the concept of the Armenian nation to have survived, an awareness of tradition must have survived. But the duduk players of today have no more inherited their traditional ways of playing the duduk from their ancestors than we have succeeded in giving a fixed definition of these traditions. Traditions have been reinvented to provide the concept of the Armenianness of the duduk with depth and support. The absence of records of these traditions has facilitated their manipulation for the purpose of ensuring their distinctive nature. The perception of pre-Soviet patterns of duduk playing has been accordingly constructed.

The post-Soviet decade has provided us with such a wealth of socio-political changes that the following words of Matossian are almost incomprehensible to us today:

> Soviet history has shown that [the use of] the mass media of communication, the technique of central planning and well constructed institutions manned by talented personnel—can "break the back" of traditional societies. It has shown that many people can set aside ethnic loyalties for the sake of ideological claims. (1962, 177)

The history of the duduk has demonstrated the robust recalcitrance of ethnic loyalties to the Soviet attempts at ridding society of "backward traditions."[1] It has shown that traditions and so-called advancements can coexist. Matossian's "mass media, central planning, and well-constructed institutions" have been instrumental in the creation and establishment of a well-defined and distinctive Armenian tradition.[2]

Eric Hobsbawm wrote that invented traditions are "responses to novel situations which take the form of reference to old situations, or which establish their own past" (Hobsbawm 1983, 2). In the absence of very early recordings of duduk music, we may assume that to a certain extent, the presupposed continuity is factitious, and the "old situations," although not without grounds, are partly fabricated. Among major obstacles to continuity were the urbanization of the duduk playing tradition and the innumerable changes effected by Soviet culture policy, which took the forms of so-called advancement and Europeanization.

But the creation of the Soviet man who was advanced and free of tradition was impeded by a misunderstanding of the strength of national identity. Instead of "eliminating nationalism as a factor in politics"[3] (Pipes 1961, 380), the Soviets provided new ways in which national attitudes could be expressed and disseminated. Marx's belief that the only true differences were class differences, and that the idea of nations would soon be extinguished has shown itself to be as distant to us today as the reality of the Soviet man. National identity has employed advancement as a means of recreating the culture of a perceived past, or to paraphrase, advancement has been the most effective tool of incorporating the past in the present.

The distinction between a real and perceived past should present no obstacle to viewing cultural memory as a tool in this process. It will however, question our conception of cultural memory. As embodied in an instrument, this memory "selects" through criteria established by ideologies and identities. The construction of place and self depends not only on communicative visual and acoustical processes such an embodiment may give rise to, but also on contexts and meanings derived from them. The adaptability of these individual context-dependent meanings to the selection process of cultural memory is determined to some extent on discourse. In this way, discourse is able to structure feeling and related meanings.

I hope I have been able to give an overview of this theory through its application on the duduk. Meanings closely related with affect, are created at funerals, special concerts, the folk ensemble, competitions, so on and so forth. Soon, they conflate into one main attribute of the duduk: its national identity. The sadness of funerals, rurality depicted in concerts, and a status raised through competitions all become qualities of national identity through the instrument of discourse. I suggest that language is able to do this through "generalizing" feeling. The example of sadness portrays this perfectly. Analogies of sadness are confused with sadness thanks to the generalizability language offers. They can then be used to create another link with national identity also known to be intrinsically connected with sadness.

A deeper understanding of traditions is indispensable for a fuller understanding of the phenomenon of nation, since the construction of the past is at the heart of identity. If cultural memory is endowed with affect as embodied in music, this construction acquires a particularly magnified validity in the members of those experiencing it. In my view, the next step should be the research into areas which may shed light on the relationship between the history of the instrument and the way in which this history is perceived. This will entail archival work and a search for older recordings, possibly from peoples' homes and radio stations. Research on the mey and balaban in Turkey and Iran will also shed light on the subject. But of greatest value will be peoples' own memories, views, and ideas of the "traditions of the old days" and how they have gradually or suddenly become the musics of today.

Notes

1. These tendencies are clearly demonstrated in the many pages that the GSE has devoted in describing the beneficial influence of Soviet advancements in the central Asian countries whose cultures were hitherto dominated by "backward traditions."

2. Matossian's mass media and well-constructed institutions, along with Westernized musical education, notation, the propagability of ensemble writing, and other so-called advancements have been instrumental in the standardization of folk songs that has facilitated the creation of distinctive traditions. I am not suggesting here that these have been the only factors which have enabled such creations. Rather that they have not in any way impeded the ideation of "the Armenian way" in the urbanized society of 1990s Armenia.

3. According to Richard Pipes, Soviet nationalities policy was a "temporary device meant to allow the regime to keep the national minorities under control at home" until such time when "the expected worldwide triumph of communism will eliminate nationalism as a factor in politics" altogether (1961, 7).

Appendix A

Transcriptions and Analysis: The Creation of Mood in Duduk Music

Selection

1. Arsen Grigorian: *Hovern Yelan*, in *Traditions of Armenia*, Nieuweigen (The Netherlands): MW Records (Music & Words)

2. Kevork Dambaghian: *Hovern Yelan*, in *World of Armenia Volume 3: Duduk*, London: Celestial Harmonies Records

3. Mgrdich Malkhasian: *Hovern Yelan*, in *Mgrdich Malkhasian: Duduk*, Los Angeles: Parseghian Records

4. Kevork Dambaghian: *Dle Yaman*, in *Music of Armenia Volume 3: Duduk*, London: Celestial Harmonies Records

5. Hovik Garapetyan: *Dle Yaman*, in *Hovig Garapetyan: Douduk*, Los Angeles: Parseghian Records

Signs Used in the Transcriptions

( )—note(s) barely audible
a—sound of air being blown
d—a very slight delay or hesitation
m—melisma
n—nasal or brassy sound
r—a repeated note effect or an unidentifiable pitch
s—slide
V—vibrato
Vv—vibrato with lower range of pitches increasingly emphasized
V^—vibrato with higher range of pitches increasingly emphasized

Transcription 1
Grigorian, Hovern Yelan
Drone=C

Transcription 2
Dambaghian, Die Yaman
Drone=C#

Transcription 3
Dambaghian, Hovern Yelan
Drone=C

Transcription 4
Malkhasian, Hovern Yelan
Drone=B

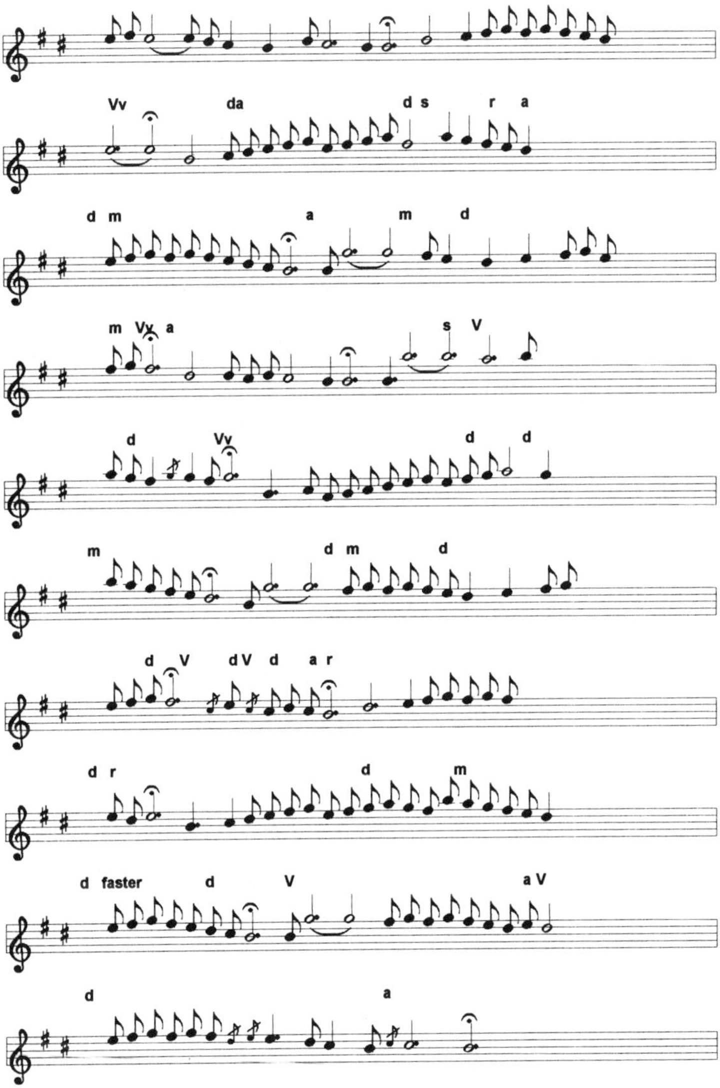
Vv da d s r a
d m a m d
m Vv a s V
d Vv d d
m d m d
d V dV d a r
d r d m
d faster d V aV
d a

Transcription 5
Garapetyan, Dle Yaman

A Note on the Transcriptions and Method

The foci of this study are two well-known pieces of music for the duduk and its drone (a second duduk) generally subsumed under the genre of "sad songs." The first is known as *Hovern Yelan* (the winds arose), though it is common to refer to it by its alternative name *Hovern Yengan* (the winds came). I have used as my sources three different recordings of this piece, one of which I have transcribed completely. The second piece (of which I have included two performances) is known as *Dle Yaman* (a name, although the word "yaman" can connote the idea of a strong-willed woman). Both pieces have, since Gasparyan's renderings, (*Hovern Yelan* in Martin Scorcese's *The Last Temptation of Christ*, and *Dle Yaman* in a CD released shortly after) become standard duduk pieces and are included in almost every CD of duduk music that has come out since. I had the opportunity of hearing them many times in contexts as diverse as funerals, the homes of duduk players, and the duduk competition described in part 3. I have used here a recording made by my teacher Arsen Grigorian which formed part of the recently released CD *Traditions of Armenia* (1998), two recordings made by Kevork Dambaghian in the CD *World of Armenia* (1995), a 1994 recording by Megerdich Malkhasian forming part of a solo-duduk music CD, and a recording made by Hovik Garapetyan in 1997. Although it is supposed that the two pieces were originally songs, I have not been able to trace these. If they once enjoyed great popularity (although I have no evidence to suppose that they did), they are certainly no longer commonly heard in song form.

The recordings were made in a studio, and are therefore very much as intended, if in fact, we can suppose that the confirmations produced during playback sessions can be regarded as confirmations of the initial intention. Occasional slips and sounds which are, according to Arsen, "normally avoided" are, for instance, present. Some of the difficulties in deciding whether these were intentional or not, were seemingly resolved by Arsen's explanations to me (at least for the case of his own recording), although the degree of subjectivity involved left a number of questions unanswered—even for Arsen's own recordings. An example is the sounding of two consecutive notes of the same pitch (sometimes melismata) separated by a tiny gap (which I have referred to as "R" in the transcriptions). These are, according to Arsen, unintentional. Why they occur at structurally similar points, (in the two passages labelled "E" and "H," for example, of transcription 1—fig. 3a and 3b below) when, to the extent that I can tell from my own experiences of performing the piece, the coincidence cannot be accounted for through technical requirements, must for the moment, remain a mystery.

Fig. 3a

Fig. 3b

My methodology has been partly determined by what is perhaps
an insurmountable obstacle for the transcriber, in the Western (or for
that matter, any) sense, of duduk pieces of the "sad song" genre, the
lack of a motor pulse. Players all agree that "duduk music does not
have rhythm" (referring to this particular genre). Passages, which are
particularly problematic, I have transcribed using a computer, by
slowing down the tempo and measuring the durations of each note.
This process however is complicated by the lack of discernible peaks
in the frequency, since the beginnings and endings of notes are characterized by very subtle dynamic changes, making the duration of notes
partly indeterminable. The problem is further exacerbated by the
drone, which often drowns the softer playing of the melody player.
Fortunately I have employed this technique only where it is necessary
and useful. Otherwise, I have tried to present notation which might
facilitate the use of my transcription for the purpose of playing the
piece (such as "d" which signifies a small delay before going on to the
next note).

Despite my aim to transcribe as prescriptively as possible, my
purpose in the transcriptions (though not for the analysis) is as much a
description of elements of duduk technique as it is a visual aid to listening. I therefore aim to find a fine balance between the extremes of a
descriptive and a clear and legible work. For example, I have considered the hindrance presented by the accurate description of certain
melismata to the ease-of-use of the transcription sometimes too great
to include them, and have therefore signified them by "M."

Problems of Transcription and Analysis

The task of any form of transcription and analysis of musical practices is by its very nature an obstacle to a clear understanding of the processes the observer is recording. This obstacle finds the possibility of its emergence in the gap between two distinct and different goals: that of the transcriber/analyst, and that of the agents determining the processes. If the object of analysis were those processes carried out by performers whose goal was, at least in part, identifiable with those of the analyst, this gap might be bridged by the necessary psychological insight, which, at least, within the narrowly circumscribed confines of the analyst's own culture, is not wholly unattainable.

The theorist's aim is always different to the performer's. As Bourdieu has pointed out (in a somewhat different context dealing with "practices" in general, not just musical), the latter's formation of concepts for the accomplishment and fulfilment of his aims has little need for stability, since it matters little to him *how* he achieves his ends, so long as he does. On the contrary, the analyst's aims *are* this very "how," and to make matters worse, he requires them to be stable or consistent. That the "how" is a matter of little concern to the performer is complemented by his desire to demonstrate it to the curious analyst, which he is, at least in the partial absence of a complete institutionalization of these processes, unable to do. What is implicit in his techniques cannot come out on questioning, since even if spontaneous conceptualization of the performer's techniques were possible through the frameworks provided by the analyst, these conceptualizations would be little more than temporary and inconsistent, as their objects are, in practice.[1]

The problems are further exacerbated by the relations between cultures which are represented by the members of this interaction. The transcriber/analyst from the West has a whole history of musical values and processes, which, unobtrusive as he may attempt to render them, are central to his ability to function. They are his instruments and have long been. The centrality of pitch/melody and beat/rhythm are as firmly grounded in his conceptualization of the musics he has to deal with, as space and time have so long been in the formation of concepts for the philosopher.

Duduk music is abundantly endowed with these obstacles. Melody and rhythm are as peripheral to good performance as they are central to players' discourse. What is particularly disconcerting is that

although players are aware of the unimportance of melodic and
rhythmic articulation in duduk music— they claim that these are vari-
able from performance to performance to the degree that the same
pieces may become unrecognizable—the very existence of the concept
of pieces being unrecognizable with respect to different renderings of
the same piece and the association of this unrecognizability with melody and rhythm, implies that melody and rhythm *do* exist as a means
of identification. Should the analyst attempt to pin down the functions
of melody and rhythm and why and how they are allowed to be unrecognizable?

Perhaps such an endeavor is bound to fail by the differences in
functionalist terms between practice and theory delineated above. In
practice, rules are interchangeable and spontaneously (and only partly
consciously) acquired only to be forgotten after they are employed. In
theory, they have to be rigid and reliable, otherwise the theory fails.

But I do not mean to sound so pessimistic, because as our so-
called poststructuralist way of thinking has amply demonstrated, there
is, after all, plenty of room for mobile and unreliable "rules" that may
serve the development of different ways and patterns of thought about
the objects of study. It follows that whatever the nature of these rules,
their very explicitness makes them fallible. The process of advancing
from their implicitness in players' performance practices to their explicitness in the analysts' appendix is also the process in which such
fallibility must arise. In other words, such rules can only be rough
guides. And this roughness is more than accidental. To use Bourdieu's
words:

> Symbolic systems owe their practical coherence, that is, their
> regularities, and also their irregularities and even incoherences
> (both equally necessary because inscribed in the logic of their
> genesis and functioning) to the fact that they are the product of
> practices which cannot perform their practical functions except in-
> sofar as they bring into play, in their practical state, principles
> which are not only coherent—i.e., capable of engendering intrinsi-
> cally coherent practices compatible with the objective conditions—
> but also practical, in the sense of convenient, i.e., immediately
> mastered and manageable because obeying a "poor" and economi-
> cal logic. (1977, 109)

This is, in fact, the logic of improvisation. And it turns our attention, before achieving a *reductio ad absurdum*, to an examination of
the function as a means of achieving the necessary framework for the

process, rather than directly investigating the process itself with the inadequate tools of musical analysis.[2]

On the surface, it may seem that to delimit the function is to look for a genesis. Why is the performer playing the piece? In the case of duduk players and folk musicians in general, at least in Armenia, as it may be with other subcultures attempting to assert their presence in the face of an expansive and all-embracing cultural hegemony, it is tempting and indeed, far from inaccurate to find the answer in this primordial assertion, the fight for a reversal of the power relation implicit in the dominant culture-subculture opposition. But of course, folk music has achieved a degree of institutionalization in Armenia which necessarily brings a number of other factors determining the genesis and setting it apart from function. Once the player has become a professional musician, has achieved his status in the community, has learned and loved the piece he is performing, a number of factors inherent in genesis are lost in the past. The function is now free to be anything within the wide-ranging capacity of the disposition of the performer. As ideology has become so central to duduk performance, the centrality of national identity is, I believe, closely related to the function of duduk performing, insofar as function is separable from all the other physical and cultural limitations of performance, and even if, in individual circumstances, the dominant ideology is not synonymous with a negotiation of identities, that is, the power relation. This latter may easily be a genesis of the ideology, but not a function of the individual performance.

Let us suppose then, that the establishment of national identity as the central function of solo duduk performances is acknowledged (as might seem fairly evident from the main body of this book). This is only an indirect function (which I shall therefore hereafter call a secondary function—a function that is at once an uncompromisable end and the presupposition that there is a more central function which is this *end's end*), as the "how" of this function is itself functions (which I shall hereafter call primary functions on account of their more "direct" relevance). Sadness and rurality for instance may fulfill these secondary functions equally well. These are, in themselves vague categories however, and have a tendency to get themselves confused with the processes which give rise to them. Their very vagueness, however, and the further interchangeability of musical and improvisatory rules afforded by this vagueness allow for the free manipulation of musical elements, by which I mean, not only what the Western-trained observer understands as the idiosyncratic schemata constructed

constructed through the interposition of melody, rhythm, etc., but also the Armenian partial appropriation of these discursive practices.

The incompleteness of conceptualization inherent in duduk performers' perceptions of their performance processes, as evidenced in their discourse, did not of course defer me from attempting to use this discourse to discern functions and goals of performances. On the other hand, neither function nor processes leading to the function, which are to some degree inseparable as already mentioned, is clarified through performers' discourse.

> So long as the work of education is not clearly institutionalised as a specific, autonomous practice, and it is a whole group and a whole symbolically structured environment, without specialised agents or specific moments, which exerts an anonymous, pervasive pedagogic action, the essential part of the *modus operandi* which defines practical mastery is transmitted in practice, in its practical state, without attaining the level of discourse. (Bourdieu 1977, 87)

Is duduk education "clearly institutionalized?" The introduction of duduk performance to the conservatory curriculum in 1978 seems to suggest that it is. But in reality, most players go only through a technicum where the degree of institutionalization is subject to argument. To the degree that it is, the institutionalization is tailored to serve performance needs within ensemble playing, while solo performance, as a free manifestation of an unusual conflation of artistic and traditional freedom, remains segregated from this realm insofar as conceptually and objectively it remains free of rules. That this is the case is evidenced by the competition and its problems as I have described them in part 3. Discursive practices around the solo duduk are only in their formation stage, if indeed they are being developed.[3]

Thus we have reduced (or expanded) the functions of duduk playing to the need for a construction of those images and depictions which are consciously and conceptually perceived to be attributes of Armenianness. Still, rurality, sadness, or any other "attributes" a performer may choose to justify his style may be manipulated, interchanged, or mixed, although perhaps, the emergence of sadness occupies a central role, at least in the recordings of the performances I have examined.

Perhaps my only claim for, at least partly, overcoming some of the obstacles I have pointed out, rest on my own experiences as performer of duduk music, limited as my ability in this domain may be, though of course, I cannot achieve a complete break with the music-educational tradition which insistently imposes its structural system on these experiences.

The Recognizability of Tunes

Speaking of duduk music in particular, Canadian guitarist Michael Brook is quoted as having said: "It's always drawn me, the kind of expression and ornamentation in Eastern music. It's not about structure, there's no architectural component to it as there is in symphonies and other Western music" (Rostan 1999). Vahan Kalstian (a duduk player, see in text) told me repeatedly that "every time a duduk player plays a piece, he plays it differently. Sometimes the very piece I play is played so differently by someone else, that I don't recognize it."

Vahan's words identify one of the most significant differences between ensemble playing and solo playing. In the former, the recognizability of the tune defines one of its central aims, in the latter, it is a matter of indifference. Indeed melodic differences between two recordings of the same piece are so fundamental that they question the validity of melody and rhythm as distinguishing elements in a piece. Let us compare the recordings of *Dle Yaman*, made by Garapetyan and Dambaghian.

The opening phrase (see fig. 4) employs three notes. The interval between the first and second is a tone in Dambaghian's recording and a semitone in Garapetyan's, whereas between the second and third note, both employ the interval of a tone. This gives Dambaghian's rendering a somewhat different mode and character to Garapetyan's. In my view the former presents a mood of sad but mixed emotion whereas the latter is characterized by a heavy gloom. Although the melodic line seems to move in a vaguely similar direction, the two melodies are clearly different. The difference is pronounced by a rhythmic ambiguity. Although in the vaguest terms, it may be argued that the two have a distant resemblance, in the former, the first note has a duration of three times the second, in the latter, five times.

Dambaghian presents new notes in the second part of the first phrase, while Garapetyan makes further use of the same three notes until considerably later. The former thus presents refreshingly new sounds, while the latter prefers to keep the music static. Though the idea of sadness comes across in both cases, it does so in markedly different ways.

Fig. 4a Garapetyan

Fig. 4b Dambaghian

The second phrase is completed by Dambaghian on a questioning and uncertain G-sharp, while Garapetyan ends it in a fatal and conclusive C-sharp. In the next phrase, Garapetyan remains highly static, whereas Dambaghian uses notes in an ornamental fashion giving the piece a certain lightness. Note how Garapetyan employs a melisma in the middle of the third phrase and how it seems to play around the same note, in a seemingly directionless manner, while Dambaghian prefers to use a larger range of notes.

At no point in the piece can one find any close melodic resemblance in the two recordings. The very vagueness of musical patterns seems as much designed to confuse the analyst's attempt at comparison as it is to ensure the presupposed ambiguity of what we call "the mood of sadness"—that is, a functional similarity.[4] In short, although function remains the same, melody and rhythm are comprised of elements which are to varying degrees *interchangeable*.

A comparison of Malkhasian's *Hovern Yelan* with Arsen's rendering produces similar results, although here certain common motives can be discerned. Comparing the first phrases, an important difference is noted by Malkhasian's use of the drone pitch to begin the piece, as compared with Arsen's fourth above drone. The former is assertive, the latter seems to hover in uncertainty. Arsen's rhythm in the first phrase seems to be ornamental in character, compared to Malkhasian's more lucid style.

Arsen ends his second phrase on the same note as he employed for the ending of the first phrase; Malkhasian uses the less certain subdominant in the first phrase followed by a relatively conclusive dominant. It is only in the use of the same pattern of notes in the third phrase that the first resemblance is noted, but the fourth phrases drift back to their separate melodic and rhythmic patterns. The degree of resemblance varies throughout the piece, reaching its highest points in the leaps of a sixth and an octave, but it is not necessary to provide here a painstaking and meticulous comparison for the reader to be convinced that the two pieces cannot be identified as the same on purely musical grounds (that is, as understood through the seemingly universal axes of melody and rhythm). This pattern of improvisation which characterizes solo playing paves a divergence from the standardizations effected by folk ensemble playing of pieces. Melody and rhythm are considered sacred in the latter, but of little consequence in the former.

The same applies for internal comparisons within a single rendering. Figure 5 for instance, compares "F" and "I" from transcription 1, where the same passage is rhythmically altered with no perceptible consistency.

Fig. 5

It may be argued that my choice of notation may exaggerate what is very roughly the same, broadly speaking, rhythmic pattern. On the other hand, we must note that the performance transcribed is a studio recording, where this particular rendering has come after a decisive number of repeated playings (in terms of both practice and performance) of the same piece within a short span of time, which will surely have served the function of "standardizing" certain schemata. In less

"institutionalized" circumstances, the differences such as those between "F" and "I" in fig. 5 will most certainly be more exaggerated.

Of-course such differences are not limited only to the rhythmic
structure (or lack of it). Fig. 6 demonstrates an analogous freedom in
the melodic contours.

Fig. 6

This may strike the reader as akin to the *ad libitum* spirit of
nineteenth century virtuosity; Liszt's piano music, for example. In
fact, however, it is a more unconscious process than the latter. This is
not a cadenza placed at some significant juncture in the musical "development"; it is representative of a wider freedom of rhythmic and
melodic articulation. There is little intention of producing a virtuoso
effect, or for that matter, an improvisatory style. That these may be the
resulting effects of such passages is related more with our perception
of such schemata than with any intentions of the performer.

But we need not dwell on this matter any longer. Any comparison of the five recordings would substantiate Vahan's portrayal of the
melodic variegation which characterizes solo duduk performances.
Central to all five recordings is the creation and communication of a
mood, often at the expense of adhering to the well-known tune. The
defining characteristic of the piece is thus its mood—its function. As
for the rest, we are left with little choice but to describe elements as
best we can, by terms such as "static," "assertive," "uncertain," "final," which for us, have meaning and thus describe sounds, but to
players, are either little more than means which might or might not be
explicitly conceptualized, or concepts which can be used inter-
changeably, depending on context, audience reaction (in the case of

live performance or reaction of producers in the case of playbacks after recording sessions), players' own moods, etc.

The Central Primary Function: Sadness, and Its "Means"

Differences in the rendering of the tune may on the surface seem susceptible to the possibility of acquiring a pronounced significance on account of the melodic standardization effected by Gasparyan's famous recordings of both. In reality, it seems a melodic standardization did not take place at all, or if it did, its effects have not manifested themselves. Rather, the standardization has been in the domain of the secondary functions which justify the duduk's status as "the most traditional Armenian instrument," that is, mood, especially that of sadness. Indeed this standardization is accompanied by the view that if Gasparyan's performance of these pieces has attempted the portrayal of its Armenianness, then he has achieved it primarily through his effective use of the element of sadness. To remind ourselves of the centrality of this element to duduk playing, I quote his words as presented in an interview by Schnabel:

> Armenian people are born into sadness. And we have heard this music from our own fathers, and we love this music even though it is sad. That is what we have inherited, and that is what comes through in the performance of our music. We can't help it. But that doesn't mean that our music is only sad music. There are many happy occasions where we play the duduk. But even on those happy occasions, we play love songs and lyric songs which have a sad aspect to them. (1998, 55)

It will have become clear to the reader that this "aspect" is both the undefinable of duduk playing (even in those happy occasions) and the object of this analysis. So far, we have established the interchangeability of melodic and rhythmic elements. But what of other elements such as texture and dynamics?

Timbre

The possibilities inherent in the manipulation of timbre for the creation of a "sad mood" cannot be overemphasized. Duduk players consider timbre to be of culminant importance for justifying the assumption that the duduk is capable of deeper expressiveness and feeling than other instruments. As is clear from my earlier argument on sadness, the duduk's capacity for creating a mood of sadness defines a basis for such an assumption. Thus timbre acquires great significance and its treatment assumes a sovereign position in the criteria by which performances are judged.

Yet the question of what makes for "fine" timbre is problematic. It is perhaps easier to isolate the sounds which are unwanted, rather than those that are most desirable and "worthy." A case in point is a certain brassy sound (mentioned in part 3) which though easy to produce, seems, on occasion, undesirable. Vahan would often excuse a player for "letting such a sound slip in" since "it happens to the best of us. Of course, Vatche Hovsepian hardly ever created such sounds, but then he was a genius." Players will often go to great lengths to make sure that their recordings of a certain piece are free of such sounds. The brassy sound is perhaps guilty of being too closely associated with dance music, and in particular with the zurna. A symbol of happy music cannot be employed to create a sad mood.

In Dambaghian's recording of *Dle Yaman*, the timbre is so well controlled that there is hardly an instant of the brassy sound. Malkhasian's *Hovern Yelan*, too, is impressively free of this problem. Arsen, however, seems less concerned by it, although the appearance of the sound is often short and not easily perceived. It is noted at locations which present minor technical obstacles such as the leaps at the beginning of passages "E," "F," and "H." Yet Arsen certainly possesses the technique to overcome such obstacles, especially in the (in these terms) ideal studio recording circumstances. Garapetyan on the other hand allows the sound, again only momentarily, at the loudest points of a phrase. In such cases, expressiveness (as manifested by dynamic variation within a phrase) is cultivated through phrasing rather than timbre. All the same, the brassy sound is short and unobtrusive. Nowhere is it allowed to impede the creation of a sad mood and is virtually continually suppressed.

These inconsistencies can be clarified by the acknowledgment of the functionality of this sound. Although players have an official (agreed) rule that such sounds should be avoided, in practice, they will only do so when they feel that it presents an obstacle to the music's sad-mood-creating potential. This "official" rule is useful only as a rough guideline, and finds pleasure nowhere more than in its capacity to present a (any) rule to the curious analyst.

According to Gasparyan, the brassy sound was a prominent feature of duduk playing fifty years ago. Arsen points out the faults of reed positioning within the mouth in the older generation, which often results in the unwanted appearance of such sounds. He argues that positioning the reed so that it maintains as little contact with the mouth as possible is the best way of avoiding the creation of the zurna-like sound. Today, Arsen's positioning is generally accepted as the norm. The advantages in terms of controlling pitch, presented by lipping, have to be compromised to avoid the creation of the brassy sound. I regard this as evidence supporting the importance of the duduk timbre and its necessity in creating a mood of sadness. But in this process, there are no "rules" for timbre, just judgments.[5]

In short, we might say that if we have failed to identify particular aspects which might serve as criteria in establishing the quality of timbre, it is due not only to the interchangeability of such criteria, but to the uncertainty of the contents of any identifications. If the brassy sound demonstrates this in a negative way, a positive example of this problem is the vibrato. Vibrati are often used as a means of varying timbre quality within the accepted range. Arsen, in advising me on the nature of vibrati, pointed out their purpose as a means of avoiding monotony: "You can play a note without vibrato, but if it's a long note, it gets boring. You have to play around with it. That's what a vibrato is." In effect, vibrato introduces color changes to long notes. Notice the locations of its appearances. Garapetyan uses it only after a short period of a note sounding without ornamentation. The first vibrato of line two, for instance, or the vibrati that come after melismata (line 2 or 3).

Again, the undeterminability of the vibrato is insuperable for the analyst. Sometimes a player makes use of it to introduce change, but at other times, it can be a useful device for concealing inaccuracies in tuning, for adjusting the awkward position of the reed, for producing the impression of being moved by the music, so on and so forth.

Dynamic Control

Although some of the performances I heard of *Hovern Yelan* accentuated the differences between piano and forte, Arsen's dynamic range is shaped as much by his reluctance to take risks as it is by his attempt to reconcile this reluctance with the expressiveness possible through it. The tendency, for instance to play the refrain softly is present in all recordings of the piece I have come across, but Arsen shows no inclination to use this as a notable contrast to other passages (although certainly he employs piano here). Loud passages are also problematic. My own difficulty in playing passage "F" of *Hovern Yelan* (especially the octave leap of the first two notes), is in retaining the same sound quality. But this problem is experienced by the finest players, as is evidenced by Arsen's production of a slightly different timbre for the high C in passage "F." Especially problematic in this sense are high notes, which have to be played loud, loudness facilitating the "unwanted" appearance of the brassy sound.

Other consequences of dynamic shading include the appearance of the sound of blowing air which I have labeled "A," especially noticeable in attempts at creating softer passages such as the refrains to *Hovern Yelan* already mentioned. Although these accentuate a wonderful dissonance effect created by the tension between D-flat and C in the refrains, they are not always intentional. Their presence in softer passages is sometimes inevitable, but no special care is taken to avoid them. Arsen explained that the appearance of air is not something to be concerned about. It often provides a method of shading and introduces new color to the timbre. The tone of this advice betrayed a "then again, if you can avoid it, do so."

The already mentioned subtlety in dynamic shading at the beginning and ending of certain long notes is evidence of the dynamic control at the disposal of the duduk player. Although this is most clearly observable when the tape speed is slowed down, the attentive listener may note this refined manipulation of sound level at the beginnings of clauses "E" and "F" of transcription 1. The significance of dynamic controllability should not be underemphasized as it provides a basis for the expressiveness associated with the instrument. Dynamic control is a vital means of conveying the sad mood, and is present in each of the recordings I have transcribed, in varying degrees.

It is also a notable fact that zurna playing is comparatively bereft of dynamic controllability. Vahan believed that this impeded its expressiveness, and made it "an easy instrument to play." One did not have to feel deeply when playing the zurna, since this instrument offered no way of manifesting such feeling, it was not capable of phrasing. If dynamic controllability is as crucial a factor in expressiveness as Vahan seems to imply, there can be little doubt that it is a necessary means of portraying sadness on the duduk.

The idea that dynamics are vital for expressiveness is conceptualized in *hoki*, which is crucial to the masterful control of dynamics. We have already noted the significance of hoki and its vitality in adding (the perception of) depth to duduk playing. According to Vahan, sadness is virtually inseparable from hoki. Thus, one of the seemingly most distinctive features of duduk technique relies on dynamic variation for the creation of mood.

The relation between hoki and dynamics is further strengthened by the duduk's reliance on blowing for dynamic control. Blowing on the duduk is carefully differentiated from blowing on the zurna. Arsen pointed out differences with zurna blowing, claiming that when playing the zurna, "one simply blows and does not need to think of how to blow." The refined embouchure of duduk players is reflected in the concept of hoki and how it is manifested in dynamic variation.

Arsen's comment about "not needing to think of how to blow" is perhaps not as limited to the zurna as might be expected. The entire network of relations between blowing, dynamic controllability, expressiveness and sadness seems a lot more reminiscent of the systems of homologies which determine practices that anthropologists have so often pointed out, than it is indicative of the rules and regulations that shape duduk playing. The significance of "official" rules is certainly not to be underestimated, but they form the subject of a different study, of a different sort of examination of psychological and educational processes, rather than what we have vaguely referred to as a musical analysis.

The Melisma

One of the most ambiguous concepts in duduk playing is that of the melisma. This "ornament" presents the analyst with numerous problems, primarily related with forming a definition for it. The players' definitions of *melismner* form a confused web of partly contradictory and vague concepts. Hovhannes referred to them as "those notes which are not clear (*hsdag*)" being uncertain of how to explain the idea of "clear." Vahan explained them as passages which use indefinite pitches, and which are highly expressive, thinking of *melismner* as closely associated with hoki. Arsen preferred to show me rather than tell me, playing parts of a dance with a number of indefinite pitches. These were either very short (no longer than two consecutive notes of unidentifiable pitch, sometimes just a single note) or a descending passage with a seemingly large number of notes of indefinite pitch played in a short space of time. These descending passages are not to be confused with sliding notes, although a melisma may very well be formed of partly sliding notes.

The elusiveness of a definition of the melisma may be partly attributable to the fact that it is not limited to passages which include indefinite pitch. Passages with slides are sometimes referred to as melismata, and sometimes not. Furthermore, the concept seems to have differing limitations, depending on the player who describes it. This may be a result of different degrees of Western influence, depending on the type and location of the player's education. If the player has graduated from the Conservatory of Yerevan, he will probably have a larger vocabulary and deeper understanding of Western terms than a player from a technicum in Leninakan. The definition of melisma has not been sufficiently standardized in the discourse of most players, so that although all are acquainted with the word, few have a clear picture of the concept.

The melisma makes use of the epiglottis (as I have pointed out in part 3) and depends on the coordination between throat, lips, and fingers. The use of the throat forms a basis for the definition of both short and long melismata; in contrast to the melismata that resemble slides which are not executed in this manner. The vague resemblance between passages which make use of slides and the Western melisma (in particular, passages which are sung to a single syllable and which are highly expressive) suggest (rather, open up room for speculation) that such passages may have constituted the original definition of the word.

Despite the broadness of these two categories (long/short and sliding), there are a number of melismner, which do not fall under either. I will here try to identify a few of these, as they appear in those sections of the five pieces I have transcribed. In Malkhasian's recording of *Hovern Yelan*, the two minor melismata in the first line are essentially single note melismata, probably executed by the use of the throat. The first melisma of the second line is a "Western" melisma but with limited sliding, while the second is the most common type, and the word is consistently applied to this type of passage. We may call it a descending melisma. Arsen's execution of descending melismata demonstrates his great confidence in approaching them, whereas Malkhasian sometimes hesitates, as for instance in line 8. The second melisma of line 9 seems to me a type of extreme vibrato. I should also note that although the passage following the second melisma of line 9 seems very similar to it, it would not be referred to as a melisma. Such cases present problems for the analyst who is interested in "definitions."

In Arsen's performance, one notices certain tendencies to avoid melismata at places which offer the opportunity. The ending of line 2, for instance, which would have accommodated a descending melisma, is furnished with a minor ornament. Also of interest is his execution of a potential melisma in line 4. Malkhasian would have certainly created a more "melismatic" sound, but Arsen's notes are *too* clear and distinct. The melisma of line 6 should not be confused with a descending melisma, despite its direction. This is closer to the Western melisma.

Garapetyan's *Dle Yaman* presents a different form of the vibrato-style melisma. He uses this well to accentuate the static nature of his performance. The melisma remains centered on the E and slides to and from an F-natural. He employs this melisma throughout the piece creating tension (but also "mood"). From such a distinction between a static and dynamic melisma, the idea of direction emerges.

I was often instructed by Arsen to think of the note to which my vibrati were directed. The concept of direction is prominent in duduk players' discourse, and must to some extent affect the shape of a melisma. But is it possible to determine in what way? Garapetyan's static melisma seems to have no direction, a matter on which little light is shed by questioning players. It sounds as static as vibrati, but the latter are sometimes employed as a means of sliding to the note above or below. Considering Arsen's *Hovern Yelan*, for instance (see transcription 1), note 10 (A-flat) of passage "B" is ornamented by a V to begin with, which transforms to a $V^\wedge$ which ends up in a B-flat. This may be considered a melisma or a vibrato, static or dynamic. Is there any need to settle these inconsistencies? For the analyst, perhaps, for the players, no.

It is advisable to note that as concepts, many of these ornaments derive their efficacy from their flexibility. They can easily be appropriated and adapted to the requirement of the moment. If a player feels that he has to change the mood of the music, he may decide to do so by using a melisma. Given the (musical) structural context in which he finds himself, he may have to adjust the concept of melisma to serve the needs of the moment. If the register in a given passage happens to be too low for a descending melisma, he may opt for a vibrato instead, but he will conceive of this vibrato as a melisma. Yet this is no more than what Bourdieu refers to as the economy of logic. Players have no time to explore all the possibilities a situation offers. They are, after all, improvising. They must therefore have a small number of apparatuses and the option to adjust these as they see fit.

In the more institutionalized setting of the West, or the folk orchestra, these options are greatly reduced together with any issues of spontaneity. Perhaps the degree of Westernization in the future will put an end to the above noted processes. On the other hand, the persistence of nationalism may cause a reactionary form of de-Westernization in certain domains (although in the light of globalization, these will probably be transitory). Whatever the future may tell, the Western influence on improvisatory practices such as solo duduk playing is at present fragmentary but somehow present. Let us consider these in greater depth.

Western Influence

Having examined the effects of Soviet culture policy at some length in the main body of this book, it may prove fruitful to compare some of the musical concepts, which shape duduk playing with similar concepts in Western musical thought. As we have noted, most duduk players today have received a Westernized musical education, which has marked their discourse by an abundance of Western terms and Westernized ideas. The Western influence in music dates as far back as the middle of the eighteenth century in Armenia, but this may only be said of classical music at a time when it was clearly separable from folk music. The use of the Russian language as the language of instruction in secondary schools (which began in 1938) was instrumental in disseminating Western thought to a far larger group of people than hitherto. Russian translations provided a wealth of material, which were not available in Armenian, bringing the West, in a sense, closer to Armenia.

The idea of melisma demonstrates how a seemingly distant concept even for Westerners paved its way into the musical discourse of duduk players. In the West it is closely associated with passages in plainchant where "the contrast between syllabic and melismatic passages is an important stylistic feature" (Arnold 1983, 2-1156), or the Jubilus, the name given to the long melisma on the final syllable of the first word "Alleluia" in the Alleluia chant, but in its wider sense it has come to be associated with the music of the near East, of the Arab world or of melodies which are of Hebrew origin (Haug 1994, 6-28). The term "melismatic" is used freely for passages which seem to make use of some of the elements which supposedly originated in this part of the world. Haug argues that such suppositions originated in the need to explain similarities, and have no factual basis (ibid. 6-28).

But to the Armenian, melismata are, as was widely believed in the West, elements of Eastern music. The term has accordingly come to denote some of those well-known "elements of the East." Indeed, comparing an Armenian melisma with the melismata of the Gregorian alleluia does not produce fruitful results. The latter are far too long, and to the listener of today do not necessarily portray any sadness. Hovhannes once compared a melisma with the sound of "someone crying" (*lats*). One may certainly claim the validity of such a comparison upon hearing Malkhasian's melismata (as for instance in transcription 3—especially lines 4, 5 and 6), but such ideas seem foreign to the Gregorian melismata.

It is interesting to note that although the term melisma must have made its entry into Armenia through the conservatory, its "official"[6] definition is only distantly related to what it has come to mean to the duduk player. But as a concept it has been adopted, modified, and shaped as dictated by the requirements of duduk playing.

The transformation of Western concepts to Armenian ones is also evident in the idea of dynamics as a necessary tool in expression. As we have noted, Vahan believed that the duduk was far more expressive than the zurna on account of its capacity for more refined use of dynamics. It is interesting to take a look at how nineteenth-century European views are reflected in Vahan's thought. It becomes clear from a consideration of nineteenth-century scholarship that the association between expressiveness and dynamics in the duduk playing world has been shaped by the presence of Western musical thought.

According to Fetis and Moscheles, "expression (in music) is the term we use for certain alterations in sound whereby notes are heard softly in some places, and loudly at other places. The change may be gradual or sudden" (Fetis and Moscheles 1837, as quoted in Blume 1994, 2-1618). Likewise, according to Nägeli, "the art of music [*Tonkunst*] and the art of language [*Wortkunst*] are bound together by a common law of expression, the law of dynamics" (Nägeli 1810, as quoted in ibid. 2-1618). According to Huber, "Dynamics is the study of interpretation and expression" (Huber 1842, as quoted in ibid. 2-1618).

Western influence has been imposed on the technical and conceptual elements present in Armenian musical activity. A wide range of Western terms have labeled existing nameless musical processes and

have affected their execution. There is no doubt that what is sometimes referred to as the melisma, or what Vahan calls the expressiveness through the duduk's dynamics were all present to varying degrees
before the advent of Western systems of thought. However, the very
alteration of the technical apparatus (the reconstruction of the instrument, for instance) and the introduction of new systems of education
(the conservatory) have perhaps effected an irreversible change which
might slowly wipe out the methods of improvisation. What I have
(following Bourdieu) called the "interchangeability" of terms and musical elements, may, through the progress of institutional rigidifica-
tion, lose its improvisatory potential and usefulness.

Conclusion

The reader who is acquainted with maqam patterns and structures will
have already noted the strong affinity between the sad song genre of
duduk music and a lot of the techniques employed in the musical practices of Armenia's predominantly Muslim neighbors. This is hardly
surprising in light of the fact that Armenia had been under Ottoman
rule for centuries. Maqams are far from unknown in Armenia (known
as *moughamats*), and a lot of duduk players will have a few maqams
in their repertoire. But the dominant factor to be considered in any
analysis of the music of this genre has to be the methods employed in
the creation of mood.

     This analysis has not aimed at providing a comprehensive over-
view of the pieces transcribed, but rather at suggesting a perspective
from which to view elements of duduk technique employed in the
recordings. It has presented aspects of technique foreign to the folk
orchestra, and which may therefore be thought of as peculiar to the
solo duduk. The importance and function of timbre, melisma, and dynamic variability have undergone certain developments on the duduk,
and some of the older recordings cited in this book provide evidence
of this. The use of pianissimo to provide contrast in repeated passages,
a method which has very much become a tradition in Western classical music, seems to have been prominent in some of the earlier recordings, but not today. The use of melismata has certainly flourished
in recent years, and the freedom in improvisation does not seem to
have been affected by years of play in folk ensembles.

     To Vahan, expressiveness is closely associated with sadness. Ex-
pressiveness is a necessary and uncompromising means of creating a

mood of sadness. I have tried to show that melody and rhythm are not vital components of this process and that the enormous differences in the use of melody and rhythm between two performances reflect the attitude that the creation of mood is far more important than the reproduction of a particular tune.

I hope this appendix has provided the reader with both an impression of some of the particularities of the duduk and a possible theoretical approach to broader issues of analysis. As I have already argued, the duduk has moved and continues to move in two clearly separable directions depending on the nature of the environment—solo or Western-style ensemble. That the influence of Europeanization has not impeded the development of the idiosyncratic elements of the instrument which are sometimes consciously promulgated, is perhaps surprising, but also highly revealing. Perhaps, on the other hand, this transitory stage of fragmented Western influence allows us the opportunity to acknowledge certain processes of musical performance which exist in both institutionalized and noninstitutionalized settings, but can be brought to our attention through the very fragmentariness of incomplete institutionalization. If nothing more, the existence of Western cultural hegemony has served as a reminder that those so-called official concepts, which players are partly aware of are not to be confused with objective structuralist rules of practice. Officialness and practice leave a gap between them that seems, at the surface, unbridged. But of course there is a bridge, and we call it "improvisation."

Notes

1. See, for instance, Lortat-Jacob's description of Sardinian performers' attempts to theorize their practices (1995). Also, an interesting account of this gap between theory and practice is to be found in Michel de Certeau's *The Practice of Everyday Life* (1984), though at a more general level this area has been well covered in the philosophical literature.

2. It is perhaps evidence of analysts' hesitance to remove themselves from the body of institutionalized musical production that Schenkerian analysis has survived for so long. If the rules of musical analysis failed to explain musical practices, new rules had to be devised. Fortunately the post-Schenkerian world of analysis has been somewhat better adapted to the logic of improvisation.

3. It is worth noting that even within the most institutionalized contexts, an inherent attribute of all practices loosely subsumed under the title "art" is what Gadamer refers to as "play" (1974), a certain leeway for improvisation.

4. Another difference between the two recordings originates in Garapetyan's drone accompaniment, which is always changing, providing a quasi-harmonic tonal centre.

5. One is reminded of Kant's "Takt" in his *Critique of Judgement* (1987). A sense of balance is an essential constituent of any artistic production, but the rules of this balance are in fact undeterminable.

6. I use the word "official" here on account of the definition given by *Grove's Dictionary of Music and Musicians* as well as that given by *The Harvard Dictionary of Music*, both of which refer only to the use of the word in academic circles, choosing to ignore its broader (and more popular) sense.

Appendix B

A Detailed Description of the Duduk and Duduk Technique

The duduk is a double-reed aerophone with a cylindrical bore, with eight fingerholes, one thumbhole, and one tuning hole on the posterior side near the distal end of the body, and a very large, bilamellate, broad reed.[1] It is made of apricot wood, and is found in Armenia and Georgia. Although Robert Atayan writes in *Grove's Dictionary of Music and Musicians* that it comes in three sizes varying from 28 cm to 40 cm, Garlen, the most well-known and perhaps only duduk maker in Yerevan, did not confirm this, stating instead that aside from the four most commonly made types, he has experimented enough to create a tiny 15 cm duduk, and could not recall the size of the largest one that has been graced by his home-workshop. The most common "A-duduk" is 35.5 cm long, with an external diameter of 2.2 cm.[2] The internal diameter is constant at 1.2 cm, only slightly dilating at the proximal end in order to accommodate the reed.

The reed known as the ghamish is 10.5 cm long, and flattened at the proximal end. Two tapes at either side of the flattened end prevent splitting, which is often the result of constant movement of the bridle, but also part of the unpredictability of organic materials. The bridle is always kept on the reed during performance at whatever distance from the proximal end is necessary for the ideal aperture diameter which it controls. At the beginning of a performance the bridle is always more proximal than later, when the aperture size needs to be reduced. The flattened end (7 cm) has been filed to make it smooth and thin, allowing the lips great control. The distal 3.5 cm (of the reed) are longitudinally furrowed, ending in a circumvolution of thread, whose purpose is to assure that the join is airtight. The bridle never reaches the furrowed area. A cap, which remains loose during performance, is attached to the bridle by a string joining one of the vertices of the bridle to one end of the cap.

The four most often played "types"[3] are the A, B, H, and D, each of these being the German name for the note that sounds when the six most proximal holes on the anterior side and the thumbhole of the corresponding duduk are blocked. The closest relatives of the duduk are probably the eastern Turkish mey and the northeast Iranian balaban.

An A-duduk can be made to play any pitch from an F-sharp to the B-natural, an eleventh above it. Although the "natural" notes, i.e., those that sound when the holes are fully blocked and no special pressure is applied by the lips, are easiest to play (the A of the A-duduk, for instance, is sharper than the tempered A, and if one attempts to play a Western scale while keeping the pressure applied by the lips consistent, one ends up a semitone higher than one should), today duduk players use the Western "tempered" scale. Since natural notes exist only in theory (pressure from the lips is constantly used to adjust pitch), it is very difficult to define a scale for the duduk. It is clear from solo performances that a far larger range of pitches is employed than just those of the diatonic scale.

Blowing

Sound quality is entirely controlled by the lips. Lips also partly control pitch. This often results in compromises between accuracy of pitch and desired sound quality. Partly for this reason, the lips are placed as near to the proximal end of the reed as possible, although opinions as to "the right way" to blow vary. Some of the players of the older generation place the reed deeper into their mouth than the younger generation, and they are often criticized for it.

The positioning of the lips around the reed is such that the vertices of the lips touch those of the reed. At no point is pressure evenly distributed throughout the oral cavity, as say, in trumpet playing, and only the lower part of the cheeks become bulbous, leaving the entire area immediately beneath the zygomatic arch unaffected by the air stream. In a great number of duduk players the lower jaw protrudes so that the lower lips occupy a more distal position of the reed than the

upper lips. The use of the masseters is easily observed on some players, especially during vibrati. The vitality of embouchure in duduk
players is such that it controls all aspects of their playing, including
possible fingerings.

Circular breathing is only used by the drone player, although the
ability to block the windpipe by use of the epiglottis while maintaining the pressure in the cheeks is used widely by melody players for
executing melismata. Clearly the roles of drone player and melody
player are not exclusive, and a player who always functions as drone
with one partner, will assume the role of melody player with another.
But certain technical idiosyncrasies for each role remain.

Positioning of the Hands and Fingering

The duduk is positioned fairly close to the body. Although it is in per-
petual motion during performance, which makes describing any angle
formed pointless, it is never held very high. The positioning of the
hands on the instrument resemble the case of smaller wind instruments, in that the holes are not always blocked by the terminal phalanges, making the hands appear large in relation to the instrument.
For most players the left hand occupies the position nearer the body
than the right hand, although the other way round is also possible.
There is no cross fingering, and the three holes nearest to the proximal
end are blocked when necessary by the forefinger, middle, and ring
fingers of the left hand, while the right hand is positioned so that it
may at any time block the next four holes. When it is necessary to
block all eight anterior fingerholes, the hands are quickly repositioned
so that the little finger of the left hand occupies the place of the forefinger of the right hand.

The exact position of the fingers on the duduk are important, as
they affect the ability to part-close holes. The palmar surfaces of the
terminal phalanges of the left hand are used, so long as the little finger
is not in use. When it is, then it is as with the right hand, the base of
the palmar surface of the middle phalanges that stops the corresponding hole. Depending on the individual shape of the player's hand, it is
often the case that the joint between the proximal and middle phalanges is used so that partial closure can be achieved by raising to the
necessary degree the middle and distal phalanges, the degree of raising corresponding with the degree of closure of the fingerhole. In the
case of the little finger however, the terminal phalanx is commonly

(but not always) used, and partial closure is effected by adjusting the position of the whole hand using the wrist, rather than moving the little finger alone.

When adjusting the position of either hand, so as to part-close certain fingerholes which require the use of the ring finger (and are particularly difficult to achieve), a slight medial rotation of the hand may take place, such that the dorsal surface becomes proximal to the body of the player. A lateral rotation is never employed.

In general, the resting position of all fingers (other than the little finger of the left hand) is on the corresponding fingerhole, so that in addition to the most distal fingerhole, only one fingerhole is left uncovered at a time. A C-sharp for instance is played (on an A-duduk) with only the forefinger of the right hand raised, and all remaining fingers in their usual position for playing an A (i.e., when blocking the six most proximal fingerholes). Variants of this style are known, but most of the younger generation are encouraged to employ this method of allowing only the minimum number of fingerholes necessary uncovered.

Notes

1. The term "broad" is used by Wanda Bryant in describing this type of reed (1990).

2. For a full list of measurements see appendix D. All measurements refer to the Armenian duduk.

3. "Types" is here translated from the Armenian *desag*, which is the term used by Garlen, as already noted, by far the best known duduk maker in Armenia.

Appendix C

Repertoire

The solo duduk repertoire consists mainly of the rendering of sad songs. Dances and Moughamats[1] (maqqams) are also played, but not very often. "Fast"[2] music is more closely related to the zurna, or clarinet, since venues where fast music is preferred require the music to be loud. The duduk is essentially a more "intimate" (Vahan) instrument, and cannot produce very loud sounds.

Solo duduk playing is heard more at funerals than at any other social occasion. Its repertoire reflects the need for sad songs at funerals. The growing recording industry is also a popular "venue" but as elsewhere only a limited number of players have access to it.

Dances are less frequently performed on the duduk, and when they are, it is usually indoors. Lively music is generally performed on the zurna or clarinet.

Ensemble duduk playing is heard mainly in the folk ensemble. Although a quartet or larger group of duduks is known, and used during funerals or at concerts, chamber groups consisting entirely of the duduk are far more developed in Georgia. In the folk ensemble, the duduk plays an important role, partly reflected by the fact that there are four duduks in most ensembles, compared with one or two of most other instruments.

A comparative study of the duduk as part of an ensemble and the solo duduk brings to light the capacity of this instrument to adapt to the necessary conditions set by Soviet culture policy, while maintaining a number of idiosyncrasies which seem to have resisted the imposition of tempered scales and motor pulses in rhythm, most of which are visible in performances at funerals.

Appendix D

Measurements Employed by Garlen in the Construction of Duduks

Fingerhole, counting from proximal end	Distance from proximal end for A-duduk, in mm.	B	H	D
First	40	35	30	24
First on posterior side	58	59	50	40
Second	34	32	31	26
Third	30	28	27	25
Fourth	31	30	30	27
Fifth	26	25	24	23
Sixth	30	29	28	26
Seventh	32	31	29	27
Eighth	30	28	27	25
Ninth	40	38	36	35
Diameter of bore (tapering towards the distal end)	11.5-11.7	12-12.5	12.5-12.7	12.5-13

Diameter of fingerholes = 9.5mm
Width of reed at widest point = 2.9mm

Appendix E

Chronology of Major Events Concerning the Armenian Nation

600 B.C.	Collapse of the wealthy kingdom of Urartu in Van (in present-day Turkey)
500 B.C.	Greek and Persian sources refer to "Armina" and "Armenians"
Early fourth century A.D.	Adoption of Christianity as the state religion; creation of phonetic alphabet, under church sponsorship
451 A.D.	St. Vardan Mamikonian dies resisting Persian Empire and its attempt at imposing Zoroastrianism. This battle is hardly mentioned in Persian sources, but is a landmark of Armenian history and symbol of Armenian identity today
Eleventh century	Invasions from Turkic tribes from central Asia
Thirteenth and fourteenth centuries	Mongol invasions stimulate Armenian migration to cities throughout Europe, Russia, and Middle East
Sixteenth century	Treaty between Ottoman and Persian empires divide Armenia into west and east
1666	First printed Armenian Bible in Amsterdam
1794	First journal of Armenian affairs in Madras
1828	Eastern Armenia comes under Russian rule
Second half of nineteenth century	Nationalist movement in literature and other cultural forms including music are developed; urban concept of ethnic identity begins to pervade rural areas

Appendix E

1877-1878	Russo-Turkish war leaves Armenian territories devastated; anti-Armenian hatred in the Ottoman Empire develops as Armenians were pro-Russian in the war
1895-1896	Nationalism on both sides results in a massacre claiming 300,000 Armenian lives
1915	Ottoman Empire uses the opportunity of world war to rid itself of a troublesome Armenian population. It is believed that between 1 and 1.5 million were executed or died on death marches across Turkey
1918	Armenia enjoys a brief period of independence
1920	Armenia voluntarily falls under Soviet rule
1921	Yerevan State University established
1965	First of a series of demonstrations in the capital paves the way for the rise of nationalism increasingly uncontrolled
1988	Anti-Azeri demonstrations lead to war
1991	Armenians vote in favor of withdrawing from the Soviet Union

Appendix F

Distribution of the
Armenian Population (1988)

Soviet Union	4,600,000
Armenia	3,100,000
United States	750,000
Middle East and Libya, Egypt, Ethiopia	475,000
Western Europe	400,000
Iran	140,000
Latin America	100,000
Canada	50,000
Balkans (Bulgaria, Greece, Romania)	50,000
Australia	25,000
Far East	12,500
Africa	5,000

Bibliography

Afanasyan, Serge. 1991, "Demographic Evolution in Transcaucasia: 1959-1989," *Armenian Review* 44: 1.

Albright, Ch. 1989, "Balaban," in *Encyclopedia Iranica*, ed. Elsan Yarshater, Routledge and Kegan Paul, London.

Alexander, Edward. 1991, *A Crime of Vengeance: An Armenian Struggle for Justice*, The Free Press, New York.

Alter, Peter. 1994, *Nationalism*. E. Arnold, London.

Anderson, Benedict. 1991, *Imagined Communities: Reflections on the Origins and Spread of Nationalism*, Verso, London.

Arnold, Denis, ed. 1983, *The Oxford Dictionary of Music*, Oxford University Press, Oxford.

Atayan, Robert. 1980, "Union of Soviet Socialist Republics: Armenia: Folk Music," in *Grove's Dictionary of Music and Musicians*, vol. 19, Macmillan Press, London.

————. 1984, "Duduk," in *The New Grove Dictionary of Musical Instruments* vol. 1, ed. Stanley Sadie, Macmillan Press, London.

Baines, Anthony. 1992, *The Oxford Companion to Musical Instruments*, Oxford University Press, Oxford.

Bedrosian, Mark. 1953, *First Genocide of the Twentieth Century*, Voskedar, New Jersey.

Berliner, Paul. 1978, *The Soul of Mbira: Music and Traditions of the Shona People of Zimbabwe*, University of California Press, Berkeley.

Blum, Stephen. 1980, "Iran: Folk Music," in *Grove's Dictionary of Music and Musicians*, vol. 9, ed. Stanley Sadie, Macmillan Press, London.

Blume, Friedrich. (ed) 1994, *Musik in Geschichte und Gegenwart: Die Allgemeine Enzyklopädie der Musik*, Bärenreiter Kassel, Basel.

Bordakian, K. B. 1985, *Hitler and the Armenian Genocide*, Zoryan Institute, Cambridge, Mass..

Bourdieu, Pierre. 1977, *Outline of a Theory of Practice*, tr. Richard Nice, Cambridge University Press, Cambridge.

———. 1993, *The Field of Cultural Production*, Polity Press, Cambridge.

Boyajian, Dikran. 1972, *Armenia, The Case for a Forgotten Genocide*, Educational Book Crafters, Westwood, N. J..

Bozalian, Ara. 1980, *The Armenians: Their History and Culture*. Ararat, New York.

Britannica Book of the Year: 1998, Encyclopedia Britannica, London.

Bronner, Simon J. 1986, *Grasping Things: Folk Material Culture and Mass Society in America*, University Press of Kentucky, Lexington.

Bryant, Wanda. 1990, "Keyless Double Reed Aerophones," *Journal of the American Musical Instruments Society* 16, 132-76.

Chorbajian, Levon, Donabedian, Patrick, & Mutafian, Claude. 1994, *The Caucasian Knot: The History and Geopolitics of Nagorno Karabagh*, Zed Books, London.

Connelly, Marie Katheryn. 1993, *Martin Scorcese: An Analysis of His Feature Films with a Filmography of His Entire Directorial Career*, McFarland, Jefferson, N.C.

Croissant, Michael P. 1998, *The Armenia-Azerbaijan Conflict: Causes and Implications*, Praeger, Westport, Conn.

Dadrian, Vahakn N. 1995, *The History of the Armenian Genocide: Ethnic Conflict from the Balkans to Anatolia to the Caucasus*, Berghahn Books, Oxford.

Dekmejian, Hrair. 1997, "The Armenian Diaspora," in *The Armenian People: From Ancient to Modern Times*, vol. 2, ed. Richard C. Hovannisian, Macmillan Press, London.

De Certeau, Michel. 1984, *The Practice of Everyday Life*, tr. Steven Rendall, University of California Press, Berkeley.

Dikötter, Frank. 1996, "Culture, Race and Nation: The Formation of National Identity in Twentieth Century China," *Journal of International Affairs* 49: 2, 590-605.

Djumaev, Alexander. 1993, "Power Structures, Culture Policy and Traditional Music in Soviet Asia," *Yearbook for Traditional Music* 25, 43-50.

Dorje, Rinjng and Ellingson, T. 1979, "Explanation of the Secret GCOD Damaru, an Exploration of Musical Instrument Symbolism," *Asian Music Journal* 10: 2, 63-91.

Dudwick, Nora. 1993, "Armenia: A Nation Awakes," in *Nation and Politics in the Soviet Successor States*, eds. Ian Bremmer and Ray Taras, Cambridge University Press, Cambridge.

Düring, Jean, Spector, Johanna, Hassan, Scheherazade Qassim, & Slobin, Mark. 1984, "Zurna," in *Grove's Dictionary of Musical Instruments*, vol. 3, ed. Stanley Sadie, Macmillan Publishers, London.

Eyck, F. Gunther. 1995, *The Voice of Nations: European National Anthems and Their Authors*, Greenwood Press, London.

Gadamer, Hans-Georg. 1986, *The Relevance of the Beautiful and Other Essays*, Cambridge University Press, Cambridge.

Garsoian, Nina. 1997, "The Marzpanate," in *The Armenian People: From Ancient to Modern Times*, vol. 1 ed. Richard C. Hovannisian, Macmillan Press, London.

Gellner, Ernest. 1997, *Nationalism*, Weidenfeld and Nicolson, London.

Great Soviet Encyclopedia: A Translation of the Third Edition. 1975, Macmillan, New York.

Greenfeld, Liah. 1992, *Nationalism: Five Roads to Modernity*, Harvard University Press, Cambridge, Mass.

Grigorian, Vardan. 1972, "The Impact of Russia on the Armenians and Armenia," in *Russia and Asia: Essays on the Influence of Russia on the Asian Peoples*, ed. Wayne Vucinish, Stanford University Press, Stanford.

Guilbault, Jocelyne. 1987, "Fitness and Flexibility: Funeral Wakes in St. Lucia, West Indies," *Ethnomusicology* 31: 2, 273-99.

Gürun, Kamuran. 1985, *The Armenian File: The Myth of Innocence Exposed*, Weidenfeld and Nicolson, London.

Haug, Andrea. 1994, "Melisma" in *Die Musik in Geschichte und Gegenwart: Allgemeine Enzyklopädie der Musik*, ed. Friedrich Blume, vol. 6, Bärenreiter Kassel, Basel.

Hobsbawm, Eric. 1983, "Introduction," in *The Invention of Tradition*, eds. E. Hobsbawm and T. Ranger, Cambridge University Press, Cambridge.

Hospers, John. 1969, "The Concept of Artistic Expression," in *Introductory Readings in Aesthetics*, ed. J. Hospers, The Free Press, New York.

Hovannisian, Richard G. 1971, *The Republic of Armenia*, University of California, Berkeley.

Hutchinson, John and Anthony D. Smith (eds), 1994, *Nationalism*, Oxford University Press, Oxford.

Jacquot, Albert. 1886, *Dictionnaire Pratique et Raisone des Instruments de Musique Anciens et Modernes*, Libraire Fischbacher, Paris.

Joffé, George. 1996, "Nationalities and Borders in Transcaucasia and the North Caucasus," in *Transcaucasian Boundaries*, eds J.F.R.Wright, S. Goldenberg & R. Schofield, UCL Press, London.

Kamenka, Eugene. 1976, *Nationalism: The Nature and Evolution of an Idea*, E.Arnold, London.

Kant, Immanuel. 1987, *Critique of Judgement*, Hackett, Indianapolis.

Kazandjian, Sirvart. 1984, *Les origines de la musique arménienne*, Editions Astrid, Paris.

Kedourie, Elie. 1993, *Nationalism*, Blackwell, Oxford.

Keldish, U. B., (ed) 1974, *Musikalnaya Entsiklopedia*, Izdatelstvo Sovetskaya Entsiklopedia, Moscow.

Kivy, Peter. 1987, "How Music Moves," in *What is Music?* ed. A. P. Alperson, Haven Publications, New York.

Kohn, Hans. 1982, *Nationalism: Its Meaning and History*. K. E. Krieger, Malabar, Florida.

Kouyoumdjian, Mesrob G. 1970, *Ntsrtsak Pararan Hayereneh Ankleren* (Comprehensive Dictionary Armenian-English). Atlas Press, Beirut.

Levin, Theodore. 1980, "Music in Modern Uzbekistan: The Convergence of Marxist Aesthetics and Central Asian Tradition," in *Asian Music* 12: 1, 149-58.

———. 1993, "The Reterritorialisation of Culture in the New Central Asian States: A Report from Uzbekistan," in *Yearbook for Traditional Music* 25, 51-59.

Levinson, Jerrold. 1990, *Music, Art and Metaphysics: Essays in Philosophical Aesthetics*, Cornell University Press, Ithaca, N. Y.

Libaridian, Gerard. 1998, *The Karabagh File*, Zoryan Institute, Cambridge, Mass.

Lortat-Jacobs, Bernard. 1995, *Sardinian Chronicles*, University of Chicago Press, London.

Lukin, Y. 1976, "The Active Nature of the Art of Socialist Realism," in *Marxist Aesthetics and Life*, eds. I. Kulikova & A. Zis, Progressive Publishers, Moscow.

Manniche, Lise. 1975, "Ancient Egyptian Musical Instruments," in *Münchner Ägyptologische Studien* 14.

Marcuse, Sibyl. 1964, *Musical Instruments: A Comprehensive Dictionary*. Country Life: London.

Matossian, Mary Kilburn. 1962, *The Impact of Soviet Policies in Armenia*. E. J. Brill, Leiden, The Netherlands.

———— 1975, "Armenia and the Armenians," in *Handbook of Major Soviet Nationalities*, ed. Zev Katz, The Free Press, New York.

Michel, Francois. 1958, *Encyclopedie de la Musique*, Fasquelles, Paris.

Nattiez, Jean-Jacques. 1999, "Inuit Throat Games and Siberian Throat Singing: A Comparative, Historical, and Semiological Approach," in *Ethnomusicology* vol. 43: 3, 399-418

Nercessian, Vrej. (ed) 1978, *Essays on Armenian Music*, Kahn and Averill, London.

Nettl, Bruno. 1983, *Twenty-Nine Issues and Concepts: The Study of Ethnomusicology*, University of Illinois Press, Chicago.

Nettl, Bruno. (ed) 1985, *The Western Impact on World Music: Change, Adaptation and Survival*, Collier Macmillan, London.

Nguyen, Phong. 1986, "Restructuring the Fixed Pitches of the Vietnamese Dan Nguyet Lute: A Modification Necessitated by the Modal System" in *Asian Music* 18: 1, 56-70.

Novello, Adriano Alpago. 1986, *The Armenians*, Rizzdoli, New York.

Picken, Lawrence. 1975, *Folk Musical Instruments of Turkey*, Oxford University Press, London.

Poché, Christian. 1984, "Zurna," in *Grove's Dictionary of Musical Instruments*. Macmillan Publishers, London.

Pipes, Richard. 1961, "Nationalities," in *McGraw-Hill Encyclopedia of Russia and the Soviet Union*, ed. Michael Florinsky, McGraw-Hill, New York.

Potschiwalow, Leonid and Wjatscheslaw Schostakowsky. 1992, *Die GUS und die anderen Nachfolgestaaten der UdSSR: Eine kleine politische Landeskunde*. Verlag Bonn Aktuell, Münich.

Qureshi, Regula Burckhart. 1997, "The Indian Sarangi: Sound of Affect, Site of Contest," in *Yearbook for Traditional Music* 29, 1-38.

Racy, Ali Jihad. 1994, "A Dialectical Perspective on Musical Instruments: The East Mediterranean Mijwiz," in *Ethnomusicology* 38: 1, 37-57.

Reinhard, U. 1994, "Türkei," in *Die Musik in Geschichte und Gegenwart: Allgemeine Enzyklopädie der Musik*, ed. Friedrich Blume, Barenreiter Kassel, Basel.

Rice, Timothy. 1994, *May it Fill Your Soul: Experiencing Bulgarian Music*, University of Chicago, Chicago.

Ridley, Aaron. 1995, *Music, Value and the Passions*, Cornell University Press, Ithaca, N. Y.

Roston, Elana. 1999, "The Duke of Duduk," in *The New Times, Los Angeles*, 12 Aug.

Sahverdian, Alexander. 1959, *Hay Erazstutyan Patmutyan Aknarkner 19-20dd (minch Sovetagan Shrchan)*, Haypethrat, Yerevan.

Schnabel, Tom. 1998, *Rhythm Planet: The Great World Music Makers*, Universe Publishing, New York.

Simpson, J. A. & Weiner, E. S. (eds). 1989, *Oxford English Dictionary*, Clarendon Press, Oxford.

Snyder, Louis L. 1990, *Encyclopedia of Nationalism*, Paragon House, New York.

Steinpress, B. S. and Yampalski, I. M. 1966, *Entsiklopedicheskii Musikalnii Slovar*, Izdatelstvo Sovetskaya Entsyklopedia, Moscow.

Stokes, Martin. 1992, *The Arabesk Debate: Music and Musicians in Modern Turkey*, Clarendon Press, Oxford.

Suny, Ronald Grigory. 1980, *Armenia in the Twentieth Century*, Scholars, Chico, Calif.

—— 1997, "Eastern Armenia Under Czarist Rule," in *The Armenian People: From Ancient to Modern Times*, vol. 2, ed. Richard C. Hovannisian, Macmillan Press, London.

Suny, Ronald Grigory. (ed) 1983, *Essays in the History of Armenia, Azerbaijan and Georgia*, University of Michigan, Ann Arbor.

Ter Minassian, Anahide. 1984, *Nationalism and Socialism in the Armenian Revolutionary Movement*, tr. A. M. Bennett, Zoryan Institute, Cambridge, Mass.

Ternon, Yves. 1981, *The Armenians*, tr. Rouben Cholakian, Caravan Books, Delmar, N. Y.

Thomson, Robert W. 1982, *Translation and Commentary on History of Vardan and the Armenian War by Elishe*, Harvard University Press, Cambridge, Mass.

Vasmer, Max. 1953, *Russisches Etymologisches Wörterbuch*, vol. 1, Carl Winter Universitätsverlag, Heidelberg.

Wald, Elijah. 1999, "A Tradition Moves On: Djivan Gasparyan Pushes Armenian Music into the Future," in *The Boston Globe*, 6 Aug.

Walker, Christopher J. 1980, *Armenia: The Survival of a Nation*, Croon Helm, London.

Weissman, Hans. 1980, "Bestattung," in *Theologische Realenzyklopädie*, vol. 5, Walter de Gruyter, Berlin.

Woodard, Josef. 1999, "Valley Life After Dark Old World, New Age Armenian Legend and His Centuries Old Instrument Find a Place in the West of the 90s," in *The Los Angeles Times*, 6 Aug.

Wright, Rowland. 1941, *Dictionnaire des Instruments de Musique: Etude de Lexicologie*, Battley Brothers, London.

Ziegler, Susanne. 1994a, "Armenien," in *Die Musik in Geschichte und Gegenwart: Allgemeine Enzyklopädie der Musik*, ed. Friedrich Blume, Bärenreiter Kassel, Basel.

———. 1994b, "Georgien," in *Die Musik in Geschichte und Gegenwart: Allgemeine Enzyklopädie der Musik*, ed. Friedrich Blume, Bärenreiter Kassel, Basel.

Index

78 rpm recording, 34
acoustical implications, 7
acoustical schemata, 8
adaptation, 8, 9, 10, 11, 12, 78
advancement, 30, 31, 40, 69, 75,
    81, 82, 83
aesthetic considerations, 14, 66
affect, 13, 14, 27, 49, 53, 83, 109,
    117
Albright, 45
Alleluia, 110
amateur groups, 33
Ancient Egypt, 42, 147
Antall, 50
anthropology, 10
apricot wood, 3, 5, 46, 115
Aram Merangulian (folk
    ensemble), 4, 38, 70, 71, 79
Aristotle, 58
Armenian cultural renaissance, 22
Armenian national culture, 29
Armenianness, 15, 41, 48, 50, 60,
    65, 66, 82, 98, 103
Armenians, ii, 3, 4, 15, 21, 22, 24,
    25, 29, 42, 48, 49, 60, 73, 123,
    124, 147
Arnold, 110
Arsen (Grigorian), ii, 4, 32, 70,
    71, 73, 75, 76, 77, 85, 93, 100,
    101, 104, 105, 106, 107, 108,
    109
Artvin, 46
asheq, 45

Atayan, 17, 31, 115
Azerbaijan, 3, 18, 21, 25, 26, 56,
    147

bagpipe, 11
Baku, 25, 41
balaban, 18, 45, 46, 47, 84, 116
baptisms, 4, 56
Berliner, 11
Black Rock, 41
Blum, 45
Bourdieu, 95, 96, 98, 109, 112
Boyadjian, 22
bridle, 78, 115
British Library, 34, 37
Bronner, 7
Brook, Michael, 41, 99
Brown, 47, 50
Bryant, 45, 118
Buni, 17, 18, 33
Bunifon, 33
burial, 53

Caucasian, 38
CDs, 4
cello, 69
cemetery, 53, 55
chogur, 45
Chukchi, 13
circular breathing, 34, 45
circumpolar culture, 12
clarinet, 56, 69, 71, 119
cleansing, 33

competitions, 15, 40, 63, 83
Composers' Union of Armenia, 32
compositional technique, 5, 31, 75
concerts, 4, 5, 15, 40, 65, 73, 78, 83, 119
Connelly, 55
conservatory, 32, 35, 39, 42, 76, 98, 111, 112
Croissant, 25

cultural homogenization, 42
cultural knowledge, 13, 14, 15
Dadrian, 25, 147
Dambaghian, 85, 93, 99, 100, 104
dan nguyet, 79
davough, 69
davul, 47
de Certeau, 113
Dekmejian, 25, 147
descending melisma, 108, 109
Dezirgenian, 39, 40
dhol, 3, 18, 37, 51, 60, 65, 69, 77
diasporan Armenian, 11
diatonic scale, 18, 37, 116
Dikoetter, 48, 50
dirijer (conductor), 69, 71
discourse, 32
Djumaev, 18, 31, 33, 42, 53, 69
Dle Yaman, 85, 92, 99, 104, 109
drone, 18, 37, 46, 51, 54, 60, 75, 92, 94, 100, 114, 117
duda, 17
dudka, 42, 147
düdük, 4, 17
duduk competition, 4, 63, 93
duduk technique, 5, 34, 39, 47, 49, 94, 107, 112
duduki, 3, 18
duduk-lute-singer, 46
Dudwick, 21, 22
During, 45, 72
dynamic shading, 106

Eastern repertoire, 38

Egyptian broadcasts, 35
embodied knowledge, 13, 14
Eno, 3, 39
Erzurum, 46
Estrada, 32
ethnic music, 32
Europeanization, 18, 30, 31, 32, 34, 35, 42, 69, 82, 113
Europeans, 35
Eyck, 50

fast dance, 64
Fetis, 111
fetishism, 10
fieldwork, ii, 4, 5
films, 4
fingerholes, 45, 46, 47, 69, 115, 117, 118, 121
fixity (of instruments), 7, 8, 9, 11, 15, 27, 48, 78
folk culture, 15, 34, 35
folk ensemble (orchestra), 4, 5, 15, 18, 24, 30, 35, 37, 42, 51, 69, 70, 72, 74, 75, 76, 77, 78, 79, 81, 83, 101, 119
folk music collecting, 24
folk societies, 7
funerals, 4, 15, 49, 53, 54, 56, 58, 60, 66, 70, 83, 93, 119

Gagaku court music, 80
Garapetyan, 85, 93, 99, 100, 104, 105, 109, 114
Garlen, ii, 4, 17, 30, 42, 46, 115, 118, 121, 147
Garsoian, 22
Gasparyan, ii, 30, 36, 37, 38, 39, 40, 41, 48, 49, 50, 55, 56, 59, 61, 63, 64, 67, 70, 71, 78, 92, 103, 105
Gellner, 23, 38
genocide, 22, 23
Georgia, 3, 18, 21, 56, 115, 119
Georgian duduk player, 48
Glasnost, 18
globalization, 16, 110

Gorbachev era, 18
Great Russian Orchestra, 69
Great Soviet Encyclopaedia, 17, 36
Gregorian alleluia, 111
Grigorian, *see* Arsen
Grove's Dictionary of Musical Instruments, 45
guan, 47
Guemuesane, 46

harmonization, 33
Haug, 110
Hebrew origin, 110
hichiriki, 80
Hobsbawm, 82
hoki, 61, 62, 63, 68, 106, 107
Hospers, 58
House of Broadcasting and Sound Recording, 36
House of People's Arts, 36
Hovern Yelan, 55, 85, 92, 100, 104, 105, 106, 108, 109
Hovhannes, 54, 55, 56, 107, 111
Hovsepian, 4, 37, 38, 41, 67, 104
Huber, 111
Hudson, 67
Hungary, 50

ideological, 10, 23, 82
idiolect, 75
idiosyncratic observations, 9
imagined communities, 14
improvization, 41, 64, 77, 96, 101, 112, 113, 114
institutionalization, 31, 37, 95, 97, 98, 113
instrument classification, 7
instrument makers, 9
Inuit throat games, 12
Iran, 18, 21, 45, 84, 125

jazz methods, 74
Joffé, 26, 147
Joze, 70
Jubilus, 110

kanun, 69
Kars, 46, 47
Keldish, 17, 33
kemantchas, 70
Khachaturian, 56, 59, 74
Khruschev, 24
Kirovabad, 25
Kivy, 59, 67
klassicheskaya muzika, 33
Komitas Conservatory, 31
korenizatsia, 23, 24, 31
Kouyoumdjian, 61
Kronos Quartet, 41

Lenin, 23, 31, 33
Leninakan, 48, 71, 108
Levin, 18, 31, 32, 33, 42, 69
Levinson, 57, 58, 59, 67
lipping, 46, 47, 105
Liszt, 102
Lortat-Jacob, 113
Los Angeles Philharmonic, 41
Lukin, 31

Madoyan, 4, 37, 38
Malkhasian, 85, 93, 100, 101, 104, 108, 109, 111
Manniche, 42, 147
maqams, 56, 112
Margaryan, 36, 37, 70
Marx, 33, 83
Marxism, 23, 31
mass society, 7
material culture, 10
materialism, 10, 12, 16
Matevosian, 73
Matossian, 31, 32, 39, 82, 84
mbira, 11
meaning, 4, 5, 8, 9, 10, 12, 13, 14, 15, 16, 18, 47, 48, 49, 51, 53, 57, 60, 65, 66, 78, 79, 81, 83, 102
melism(a), 32, 34, 40, 48, 56, 62, 63, 67, 86, 93, 94, 100, 105, 107, 108, 109, 110, 111, 112, 117

mey, 3, 18, 29, 40, 45, 46, 47, 84, 116
Moscheles, 111
moughamats, 56, 112
mount Ararat, 39
Mus, 46
musical composition, 31
musical culture, 9
musical education, 36, 37, 42, 76, 84, 110
musical instruments, 7, 9, 10, 11
musical norms, 9
musicology, 8

Nägeli, 111
Nagorno Karabagh, 22, 24, 25
national celebrations, 65
national culture, 27, 35, 48, 65, 66, 74
national feeling, 5, 18, 24
national identity, 3, 15, 18, 22, 30, 35, 39, 41 48, 49, 50, 65, 74, 78, 83, 97
National Radio, 63
national sentiment, 66
National Sound Archives, 34
nationalism, 18, 21, 22, 23, 24, 25, 26, 27, 33, 35, 39, 48, 50, 83, 84, 110, 124, 147
nativization (korenizatsia), 23
natsionalizm, 33
natsionalnaya muzika, 33
natsionalnaya politika, 33
Nattiez, 12, 13
nay, 42, 46, 147
Nettl, 50
Nguyen, 79
nineteenth-century Romanticism, 29
notation, 18, 37, 38, 70, 76, 77, 84, 94, 101

ölcü, 46
organological artifacts, 9
organological literature, 8
organological structure, 7, 8

organological thinking, 9
organology, 8, 11
ornaments (and ornamentation), 34, 40, 41, 99, 105, 109
Ottoman Empire, 21, 124

Paronian Theatre, 32
Pavlich, 48, 54, 57
People's Artist of Armenia, 39
Perestroika, 18
performers, 9, 32, 63, 95, 98, 113
Persia, 21
Philharmonic Society, 31
photographs, 8
physical characteristics (of instruments), 7, 8
physical structure, 8, 9
physiological abilities, 9
Picken, 17, 46, 47
Pipes, 83, 84
pitch, 34, 46, 47, 77, 79, 86, 93, 95, 100, 105, 107, 108, 116
players, 4, 8, 32, 34, 35, 36, 37, 38, 40, 41, 49, 53, 54, 55, 61, 62, 63, 64, 66, 69, 70, 71, 72, 73, 75, 76, 77, 78, 82, 93, 95, 96, 97, 98, 102, 103, 104, 106, 107, 108, 109, 110, 112, 113, 116, 117, 119
playing technique (s), 7, 9, 12, 29, 45, 46, 48, 51, 81
Poché, 66
Politburo, 40
polysemy, 10, 11, 13
postmodernism, 12
Potschiwalow, 25
pre-Soviet history, 18
procession, 55
Professional Union of Art Workers, 53
propagability (of music), 74, 75, 81, 84
Prudian, ii, 4, 32

qaval, 45
Qureshi, 13, 14, 15

rabab, 70
rabis, 4, 48, 53, 62
racial nationalism, 48, 50
Racy, 8, 9, 11, 12, 13, 15, 16
radio, 24, 33, 34, 63, 73, 75, 79,
    84
reconstruction (of instruments),
    18, 33, 42, 69, 112
recording artists, 33
recording studio, 60
recordings, 3, 8, 29, 34, 37, 39,
    40, 47, 60, 66, 73, 82, 84, 92,
    93, 98, 99, 100, 102, 103, 104,
    106, 112, 114
reed, 3, 30, 45, 46, 69, 78, 80,
    105, 115, 116, 118, 121
reflection of social structures, 9
Rice, 43, 69
Ridley, 66
right of self-determination, 23
ritornelli, 47
Rostan, 99
rural areas, 29, 123
rurality, 15, 66, 83, 97, 98
Russia (and Russians), 17, 21, 35,
    62, 123
Russian influence, 29

sadness, 5, 15, 16, 34, 40, 48, 49,
    50, 55, 56, 57, 58, 59, 60, 66,
    83, 97, 98, 99, 100, 103, 104,
    105, 106, 107, 111, 112, 147
sarangi, 13
Sarkissian, 72, 74
Sayat Nova, 75
Saygun, 46
Schnabel, 30, 67, 103
Schostakowsky, 25
Scorcese, 3, 92
Scotland, 11
semiological, 12
shawm, 37
shepherds, 36, 40, 65
Shona, 11
shvin, 69
Siberian throat singing, 12

skiladiko, 53
slides, 40, 56, 108, 109
Snyder, 18, 21, 25, 43, 147
sound ideals, 9
Soviet culture policy, 30, 31, 75,
    79, 82, 110, 119
Soviet ideology, 30
Soviet rule, 24, 29, 38, 66, 69,
    124
Spendiarov Academic Theatre of
    Opera and Ballet, 32
Stalin, 31, 35
Stokes, 35, 79
Sumgait, 25
Suny, 22, 39
symbolicity, 8, 15

taghoumi bureau, 54
Taloul Altounian ensemble, 70
technicum (s), 35, 42, 76, 77, 98,
    108
technology, 8, 61
television, 73, 74, 78, 79
temperament, 32, 67
The Last Temptation of Christ, 3,
    55, 92
Thomson, 22, 25, 147
thumbhole, 45, 46, 115, 116
Tigranian, 75
timbre, 59, 77, 78, 103, 104, 105,
    106, 112
Tonkunst, 111
traditional costume, 39
traditional dances, 39, 65
traditional dress, 65
traditional music, 31, 33, 36, 41,
    65, 74
traditions, 66, 73, 81, 82, 83, 84
Transcaucasian economic union,
    41
tuning hole, 45, 115
Turkey, 3, 18, 21, 29, 34, 45, 79,
    84, 123, 124
Turkish duct flute, 17
Turkish tunes, 34
twelve tone style, 72

UNESCO prizes, 40
urban areas, 29, 36, 38, 66, 74
urban population, 11, 35, 74
urbanization, 36, 38, 74, 82

Vahan, ii, 37, 39, 53, 56, 57, 59,
   61, 62, 70, 78, 99, 102, 104,
   106, 107, 111, 112, 119
vibrati, 34, 37, 56, 105, 109, 117
Vladimir horn players, 69

wake, 53
Walker, 21, 22, 60
weddings, 4, 57
Western hegemony, 63
Western influence, 108, 110, 111,
   113

Western terms, 108, 110, 111
Woodard, 39, 40
world music, 11, 39, 61, 78
Wortkunst, 111

yasti balaman, 3, 18
Yerevan, 4, 32, 35, 39, 54, 108,
   115, 124
Yerevan State Conservatory, 4
yerki bar, 73
Young Turks, 22, 25, 147

Zimbabwe, 11
zurna, 33, 34, 36, 37, 47, 49, 56,
   59, 60, 66, 104, 105, 106, 107,
   111, 119

About the Author

Andy H. Nercessian began his musical career as a pianist playing in venues throughout Europe as recitalist or as soloist performing with orchestras. Although he continues to play today, his interest in the philosophy of music and love for the little-heard musics of non-Western cultures have fostered a special interest in ethnomusicology. Postgraduate studies at Cambridge, UK, and research in Armenia (his country of descent), brought to light a number of academic works whose subjects range from topics in organology to theory of the perception of music. Nercessian also supervises a number of undergraduate music courses at the University of Cambridge.